INVASIVE SPECIES

Invasive Terrestrial Animals

INVASIVE SPECIES

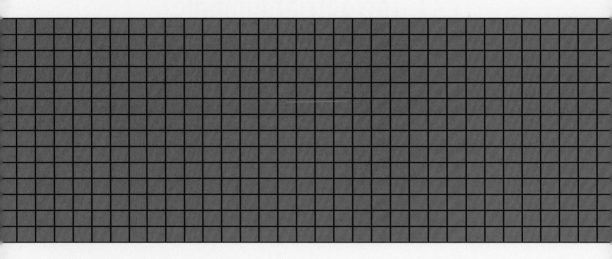

Invasive Aquatic and Wetland Animals
Invasive Aquatic and Wetland Plants
Invasive Microbes
Invasive Terrestrial Animals
Invasive Terrestrial Plants

INVASIVE SPECIES

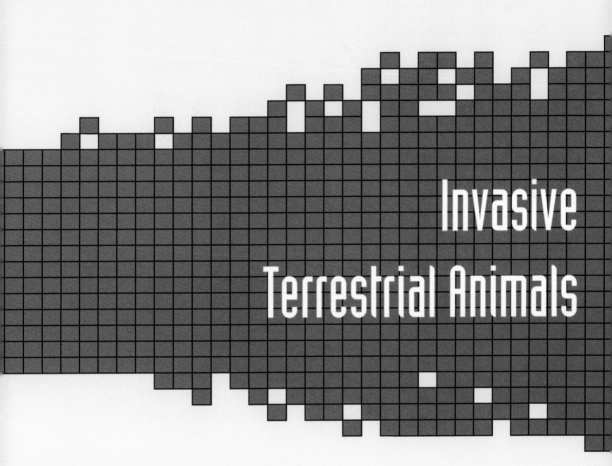

Invasive
Terrestrial Animals

Suellen May

CHELSEA HOUSE
PUBLISHERS

An imprint of Infobase Publishing

Invasive Terrestrial Animals

Chelsea House
An imprint of Infobase Publishing
132 West 31st Street
New York NY 10001

Library of Congress Cataloging-in-Publication Data

Invasive terrestrial animals / Suellen May.
    p. cm. — (Invasive species)
Includes bibliographical references and index.
ISBN 0-7910-9127-9 (hardcover)
1. Introduced animals—Juvenile literature. I. Title. II. Series: May, Suellen. Invasive species.
  QL86.M39 2006
  581.7'6—dc22

                   2006009832

Text design by James Scotto-Lavino

Cover design by Takeshi Takahashi

Printed in the United States of America

Bang EJB 10 9 8 7 6 5 4 3 2 1

This book is printed on acid-free paper.

TABLE OF CONTENTS

1 The Natural World of Terrestrial Animals 7

2 The Rise of Invasive Terrestrial Animals. 26

3 The Red Imported Fire Ant: Marching
Across the South 37

4 The Brown Treesnake: Eating Guam's Birds to
Extinction 48

5 The Wild Boar: Pigging Out in American Fields and
Forests 56

6 The European Starling: Blame It on Shakespeare 64

7 Emerald Ash Borer: Anything But a Gem 68

8 Formosan Subterranean Termite: Building Nests,
Recruiting Soldiers 73

9 Winning the Battle Against Invasive Terrestrial
Animals 82

Notes 95

Glossary. 97

Bibliography 99

Further Reading 103

Index 106

The Natural World of Terrestrial Animals

Terrestrial animals include all nonplant organisms that live on land. Most people think of fuzzy mammals when they hear the word animal, but the animal kingdom includes everything from insects to sponges and a host of other creatures.

Life evolved from the ocean to the land. Terrestrial life required a development that would enable these animals to be upright since they did not have the natural buoyancy of water to support them. A skeleton provides the strength of bone or a hardened exoskeleton to support the animals on land. Without an internal or external skeleton, an animal must creep or writhe over surfaces by contracting muscles of the body wall.[1]

The presence of a skeleton is an identifying feature of terrestrial life, although not all terrestrial animals have a skeleton. The earthworm does not have a skeleton like humans, nor does it have a hardened exterior exoskeleton. Instead, the earthworm has a hydrostatic skeleton that consists of pressurized fluid inside the worm's body. The purpose is the same, however—to give support to an animal's structure.

A striking difference between terrestrial animals and their counterparts in the plant kingdom is that animals can move around. Not being rooted in the ground, animals can flee their predators or hunt prey. One challenge that terrestrial animals face is finding food rather than making their own food as chlorophyll-containing plants do. The pure white arctic fox (*Alopex lagopus*) must cross nearly 600 miles (960 kilometers) of pack ice in 40-below-zero conditions during the winter for its food: rodents or mammal carcasses. Instead of going dormant as plants do, animals must find another way to deal with seasonal changes by either hibernating or migrating.

It is impossible to summarize terrestrial animals in one chapter but presented below are a few of the more remarkable groups and some unique characteristics they possess. First, let's begin by putting the animal kingdom in the context of the five kingdoms of life.

THE FIVE KINGDOMS OF LIFE

All life is grouped into categories based on similarities. Until very recently, the kingdom was the broadest category that life was placed into. Since 1969, the scientific community has recognized five kingdoms: Monera, Protista, Fungi, Plantae, and Animalia. Prior to 1969, there were only two recognized kingdoms: Plant and Animal. The kingdom **Monera** includes bacteria and blue-green algae. The kingdom **Protista** includes mostly unicellular organisms including algae and amoeba. The kingdom **Fungi** includes mushrooms, molds, and mildews. The kingdom **Plantae** includes mosses, ferns, and flowering plants. The kingdom **Animalia** is broken down into **coelenterates**, which are organisms with a hollow body cavity such as a jellyfish; **annelids**, which are worms with segmented bodies; **arthropods**, which have exoskeletons and jointed legs, such as grasshoppers, lobsters, and spiders; and **chordates**, which have a nerve cord and usually a backbone, such as humans and other mammals, birds, reptiles, amphibians, and fish (Figure 1.1).

In 1969, Robert H. Whittaker, a scientist from Cornell University, created this five-kingdom classification. One criterion

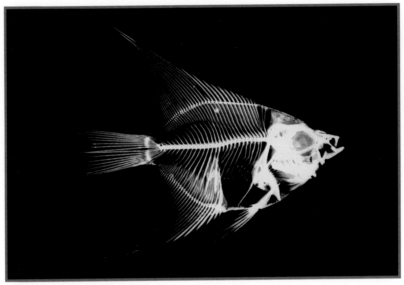

Figure 1.1 A skeleton provides support to the bodies of many terrestrial animal species. Aquatic animals, on the other hand, are able to use water as a means to buoy their bodies. Skeletons can be internal or external.

for the distinction among kingdoms was nutrition. Plants make their own food by photosynthesis. Fungi and animals are **heterotrophs**. Heterotrophs cannot derive energy from sunlight or inorganic chemicals so they must feed on other life-forms; they obtain nutrition from organic molecules. For example, most fungi are decomposers that invade their food source, secreting digestive enzymes, and absorbing the small organic molecules produced by digestion.[2]

Whittaker's five-kingdom system is currently being revised to expand the number of kingdoms and put them under another category of "superkingdoms" referred to as domains. The domains are Bacteria, Archaea, and Eukarya. The reason for creating an additional taxonomic category of the domains is due to the discovery that unicellular organisms without a nucleus (Bacteria and Archaea domains) are far more varied than once thought. Multicellar organisms with a nucleus (Eukarya domain) are plants, animals, fungi, and protists.

THE ANIMAL KINGDOM: VERTEBRATES AND INVERTEBRATES

The animal kingdom includes **vertebrates** and **invertebrates**. Vertebrates are animals with backbones. The vertebrates include fishes, amphibians, reptiles, birds, and mammals. Invertebrates are animals without backbones and include sponges, corals, lobsters, and insects (Figure 1.2). Grasshoppers are one type of terrestrial invertebrate. Whereas the skeleton of a vertebrate lies beneath the skin and muscle, the exoskeleton of the invertebrates provides a supporting framework for the tissues within and provides a surface for the attachment of muscles.

Figure 1.2 A mollusk is an invertebrate and does not have an internal skeleton like humans. Instead, a mollusk such as this green snail has a hardened exterior to lend support to its body.

This exoskeleton is only covered by the eyes, antennae, legs, part of the digestive tract, and the respiratory surfaces.

In the next sections we will look at some representative invertebrates—the insects and the worms—followed by some representative vertebrates—the mammals, amphibians, and reptiles.

Bugs: Earning Their Legs

May Berenbaum spent the first half of her life hating bugs. Now she educates and entertains people about insects. As a professor of **entomology**—the study of insects—at the University of Illinois, she was approached to do a Saturday morning segment on insects for a radio show. Knowing the opinion most people have of insects, Berenbaum was hesitant but agreed. The show was called *Those Amazing Insects.* To her surprise, the show was enormously popular. Each week she would highlight insects such as bedbugs or mayflies. She developed a following. Occasionally she was stopped on the street and asked to identify interesting creatures that people had come across. Other people wrote the station with questions. The experience led Berenbaum to conclude that people really are curious about insects when given just a little bit of information. And certainly we should be, considering they are all around us.

The role of insects in the natural world

Insects are identified by their three-segmented bodies, their six legs, and the fact that those legs are jointed (Figure 1.3). Identification of insects can be much more difficult than looking for these three characteristics. For example, insects have different life-forms: larva, pupa, and adult. Larval forms, such as the maggot, lack legs but are still insects; they are just waiting to get to the part of their life cycle when they will have legs.

Insects are crucial to the survival of humans. If all the insects were to disappear from the earth—if there were none to pollinate plants, serve as food for other animals, and dispose of dead organisms—virtually all of the terrestrial ecosystems on earth, those webs of life consisting of communities of interdependent organisms, would unravel and cease to function.[3]

Insects pollinate plants, disperse seeds, supply food, and provide defense against other predators. Without insects, many fruits and vegetables would disappear. Insects are an integral part of the food chain, providing nutrients for animals that cannot consume plants. Grasshoppers are well known for their consumption of plants. When grasshoppers in turn become a source of food for mammals that do not consume plants, they bring those plant nutrients into the food chain.

Insects are nature's mighty recyclers. While in Colombia, a scientist had a firsthand account of this recycling of dry-

---

An Insect by Another Name

Even scientists make mistakes. The larvae of *Microdon* make their home in ants' nests; they eat the ant leavings and grubs. Ants are an organized bunch that do not like intruders. As such, they would sting and bite the *Microdon* larvae. The larvae would not be defeated however and accommodated itself with the evolution of a tanklike and featureless exterior. Scientists examined this creature and deemed it a mollusk as a result of its appearance. They had no idea that the *Microdon* would eventually pupate and grow legs. Once the scientists discovered that *Microdon* were just baby flies, they properly placed them in Class Insecta.

Figure 1.3 Insects have a body segmented into three parts as shown. To be classified as an insect, an animal must also have six legs, and each leg must have a joint.

wood termites. Gilbert Waldbauer, professor of entomology at the University of Illinois, tells of observing recycling by dry-wood termites, while he was on sabbatical with his family in Columbia, South America. He was hoping to use the wooden desk in his rented home, but also noticed hordes of winged termite kings and queens flying around at night. When

Waldbauer put his hands on the desk, the entire desktop caved in. The desk had been hollowed out by dry-wood termites and was held together by only a thin shell of wood and paint. Another dramatic account of a severe termite infestation occurred in Champaign, Illinois, when a refrigerator fell through the first floor of a dwelling into the basement. Insects, such as termites, break down plant parts so that nutrients can be incorporated more quickly into the soil.

Surprisingly, termites cannot break down the main ingredient in wood and dead plants all by themselves. Termites enlist the help of microorganisms, such as bacteria and protozoans (members of the kingdom Protista) to digest cellulose. These microorganisms live in the termite's hindgut of their digestive system. The microorganisms benefit by getting a cozy home with food delivered directly to them. Termites would literally starve to death without these organisms even if they had a steady supply of wood. The microorganisms are equally dependent on the termites for their survival. This relationship is often referred to in the study of ecology as **mutually beneficial** (or **mutualism**). We will return to examining these interrelationships later in the chapter.

Ants, on the other hand, employ slavery to keep their communities running smoothly. These "slaves" do all the work in the community, whereas the males and fertile females do no work. The infertile workers make the nests and feed the larvae. When the ants must migrate because their current home is found to be unsuitable, the slaves determine where the new nest will be and carry their masters in their jaws to the new location.

Ants will steal slaves from other colonies. Honeypot ants (*Myrmecocystus spp.*) often attack neighbors and carry off their workers.[4] Some ant species actually stage an attack and steal the cocoons and use these young ants as their workers. The most clever ploy is to spray a slave colony with an alarm signal; the ants acting as guards flee in fear and then the thieving ants rush in to steal the cocoons.

Insect reproduction

Insects have creative ways to attract the opposite sex. Their ploys include making love potions and singing romantic serenades. These love potions are known as pheromones. Pheromones are chemicals released by animals to influence behavior or development. Next time a mosquito lands on your windshield

Firefly Trickery

Male fireflies must be particularly careful not to get too swept up in their flashing mating rituals. A predatory female impostor can be fatal to male fireflies. *Photurus* is a predaceous type of firefly where the female eats fireflies from the group *Photinus* by mimicking the flashing pattern of female *Photinus*. The unsuspecting males fly to this predaceous female firefly and the duped males are then eaten. In addition to the female *Photurus* getting a meal, ingesting the male enables the female to consume a steroid chemical contained in her prey that is repulsive to her predators, such as birds and spiders. *Photurus* females have the best of both worlds: They get to eat what to some would be foul-tasting prey, and in return become repulsive to their own predators.*

*James Wangberg. *Six-Legged Sex: The Erotic Lives of Bugs.* Golden, Colorado: Fulcrum Publishing, 2001, p. 24

or window, look to see if it is male or female. A male has tiny hairs on his antennae. These hairlike structures catch the molecules of the pheromones of the female. Insects also use such infochemicals to find food, mates, and sites for their eggs and young.

These infochemicals are responsible for the interactions among plants, herbivore insects, and predatory insects, such as wasps. If left to chance, a wasp without the help of pheromones to guide her could spend her entire life searching for a host on which to lay her eggs.

Most people are aware of the noise a grasshopper makes to serenade a mate, but this type of ploy is not limited to just one species of insect. Moths and waterbugs also use body parts to create song in the hope of attracting mates.

Another way that insects can attract mates is with a flashing pattern. Fireflies are actually not flies but beetles and are able to light up their rear ends when two chemicals (luciferin and luciferase) are combined. When a male lights up, it is not simply to lure a female but also to elicit a flashing reply from her so he can recognize her and know her whereabouts.[5] Each firefly has a signature flash that varies in intensity, color, frequency, and duration. Fireflies are able to communicate sexual preferences through these flashes. Yellowish light indicates a preference for early-morning sexual activity, whereas fireflies with greenish hues prefer late-night festivities. The combination of flashes creates a rich repertoire of courting between males and females.

THE BENEFIT OF WORMS TO THE SOIL

If you happen to be in the picturesque city of Fort Collins, Colorado, you may get lucky enough to see the Wormbulance. From a distance it looks like nothing more than an ambulance and actually, it is. But it is clear this is not a traditional ambulance by the scrawl of "Wormbulance" on the side and an

Figure 1.4 Earthworms are terrestrial animals without an internal or external skeleton; therefore, they must writhe over and under objects to get around on land.

accompanying sign that says, "Visualize global worming." This ambulance may no longer transport the injured, but it does transport a hefty supply of soil and worms.

John Anderson is the owner of the Wormbulance and he is passionate about composting. He knows we would be up to our necks in garbage without the majestic earthworm (Figure 1.4). Anderson educates people about the benefits of worms. Worms are the great decomposers with approximately one pound of worms eating half a pound of food scraps daily. The waste product of the worms, known as castings, is highly regarded as a soil amendment, which is a material that aids plant growth by improving soil quality. Anderson sells both the worms and the composting equipment. Composting helps redirect food that would take up space in a landfill and uses it to make a valuable resource.

Of course, worms don't need special composting bins to do what they do in nature. Have you ever walked across a particularly bumpy lawn? That bumpiness is from earthworms in the soil. The feeding and burrowing of worms incorporates organic matter into the soil. It is similar to a baker making a cake; all the ingredients are in the bowl, but it needs to be mixed to become batter. Earthworms help mix nutrients and oxygen.

MAMMALS

The world's list of mammals is about 5,000 species long, but 3,000 more may be waiting in the wings.[6] Scientists believe there are still many to discover. Back in the Victorian era, explorers discovered roughly five hundred of these warm-blooded creatures per year, including the mountain gorilla in Africa. New mammals are discovered today at a rate of roughly 100 per year. In 1992, strange horns were seen in the homes of Laotian hunters living in Southeast Asia. Scientists, not recognizing the horns, were curious and began to search for the animal from which those horns came. After two years of searching, they found the mammals living in wooded mountains. This animal is called the saola (*Pseudoryx nghetinhensis*), a bridge between oxen and antelopes. This forest-dwelling ox is considered one of the world's rarest mammals. It is currently listed as endangered due to hunting and loss of forest habitat due to logging and conversion to farmland. The discovery of the saola reminds scientists how often we come close to losing a species before we have even discovered it.

AMPHIBIANS AND REPTILES

Male iguanas might be considered cold-blooded but they like to entice their females by doing push-ups. The front legs bend and straighten rapidly on this lazy-looking reptile.

Iguanas live long lives and develop a memory. These iguanas were once hunted, like many other creatures on the Galápagos Islands. Now that the hunting is forbidden, much of the animal life on the archipelago is very tame. The plentiful iguanas have become so friendly that if you stick out a leg and lean back a bit, the iguana will crawl up your body. Island residents that lead these trips now discourage this type of interaction yet the iguanas' lack of fear of humans persists. This lack of fear could be disastrous if a predator were to show up on the island.

For the tortoises on the Galápagos, fear is not so easily forgotten. These tortoises live to be older than 100 years. Live tortoises were considered meat for those who sailed through the region. The living tortoises were taken off the islands and stacked up on ships to provide food during the voyage. Tortoises were also used for target practice and even today there are tortoises with bullet holes in their shells. These very tortoises are the ones that will groan if humans come too close. When we invoke the name of a creature that never forgets, maybe we should say "he/she has the memory of a tortoise," rather than "the memory of an elephant."

THE FOOD CHAIN: WHO EATS WHAT. . . . OR WHO?

Organisms in the Animal Kingdom do not contain chlorophyll and therefore are not able to make their own food. Yet, the creation of flesh, antennae, and beaks all require the nutrients contained within plants.

The food chain builds on these levels of who eats what, starting with plants. All terrestrial animals are interconnected and rely on others for their populations to remain healthy. Some terrestrial animals get their energy from consuming only plants. These **herbivores** have special digestive systems to enable them to eat plants. Large herbivores include cows and elk; medium-sized herbivores include goats, and small ones include squirrels and mice. Omnivores or carnivores will eat the herbivores so there must be enough herbivores in the ecosystem to meet the needs of these other eaters.

Omnivores eat both meat and plants and some will hunt for their food while others scavenge for dead animals. Large omnivores include humans and small ones include pollinating insects.

Carnivores kill and eat other animals; they eat both herbivores and omnivores. Carnivores are important in an ecosystem because they keep the population of the other animals in control. Large carnivores include wolves and small ones include snakes and hawks.

GETTING ALONG: THE INTERRELATIONSHIPS AMONG SPECIES

Terrestrial animals have a variety of interactions with individuals of their own species, other species, and their environment. Some terrestrial animals provide some benefit to another organism while getting something out of it themselves as is the case in mutualism. Mutualism is a relationship where both species benefit. It is also referred to as a symbiotic relationship. Species may exchange food or provide shelter, but may be able to both live independently. **Parasitism**, on the other hand, is a relationship where one gains and the other loses.

Brood Parasitism in Birds

Darwin, the great founder of the theory of evolution, believed that there was no commonwealth, or "common good" in the natural world. Self-interest was the name of nature's game. One great display of this is in brood parasitism. Birds will push out the young from another bird species' nest and replace it with their own eggs. The host bird unknowingly rears the brood or nestlings of the other species.

As evolution would dictate, birds grow wise to the species of birds that tend to hoodwink them. In Africa, there are roughly 30 or more species of parasitic birds; in North America there is just one, the brown-headed cowbird (*Molothrus ater*). African birds tend to be much more suspicious of young birds in their nests that make a noise different than what they are accustomed to. The North American birds victimized by the cowbird are usually unable to detect these foreign nestlings and will feed them without hesitation.

Change the natural environment and this evolutionary wisdom is lost. The village weaverbird (*Ploceus cucullatus*) living in Africa rejects most cuckoo birds (*Cuculus canorus*), which are highly parasitic birds. The village weaverbird, however, was introduced to the Caribbean back in the eighteenth century and has since lost the ability to recognize the cuckoo bird eggs. If the weaverbird in the Caribbean were to ever meet up with the parasitic cuckoo bird, the weaverbird would be at a disadvantage.

Parasitic birds compete better if they have better memories. Species will evolve to be more fit or more competitive, according to evolutionary biology. A keener memory for a brood parasite helps them to find all those eggs they have in different nests. In Jamaica, the shiny cowbird (*Molothrus bonariensis*) is an **obligate brood parasite**, meaning that it imposes the chief duties of raising its young—building the nest, incubating the eggs and rearing the young—on another bird. The female shiny cowbird is solely responsible for rearing the young and with estimates of eggs per season at 60 to 120, it is easy to understand why memory is so important; the female bird must remember where she put her eggs.

Parasitism and Humans

Most people consider themselves at the top of the food chain, consuming other animals and plants. Parasitism, however, exists between humans and other organisms. Parasitic relationships provide a benefit strictly for the parasite to the detriment of the

Figure 1.5 A botfly maggot often finds a host to feed upon until it matures to the next life stage. A relationship where the host suffers and another species, such as the botfly maggot, benefits is called parasitism.

host; the parasite generally does not kill its host. Jerry knows this better than most other Harvard biology students. Jerry was a graduate student enrolled in a field course in Costa Rica. A few weeks before Jerry planned to return to Massachusetts after finishing his course, his head itched and he noticed a small lump. After a few days of itching and worrying, one of his fellow students, a medical entomologist, agreed to examine the lump. The entomologist noticed a tiny hole in the lump and within the hole was a wiggling insect spiracle, a snorkel-like tube that the larvae poke through the host's skin. A squishy botfly maggot (*Dermatobia hominis*) was living inside the skin on his head and snacking on his flesh (Figure 1.5). Jerry panicked and after calming down asked for the maggot to be removed. As with most things, it was easier said then done. The entomologist informed

Jerry that the maggot had anal hooks that made removal difficult. A tug of the maggot would cause the anal hooks to dig in deeper; pulling even harder will cause the maggot's body to break in two with the part that is still embedded possibly causing an infection. A surgeon could remove the maggot, but there were few that Jerry felt comfortable with in the rain forests of Costa Rica.

Jerry learned to accept his larva. Most of the time the larva's presence was painless except when Jerry went swimming. Submersion in water cut off the larva's air supply and the insect thrashed around inside Jerry's head. Jerry returned to Massachusetts and declined medical intervention to remove the maggot. Jerry decided to let the larva complete its life cycle: once the larva matured, it would leave Jerry's head. Jerry enjoyed the notion of being at the bottom of the food chain for once where small creatures feed off of him instead of doing the consuming himself.

While at a baseball game in Boston, Jerry felt a stir. Protruding from the goose-egg lump on his head was a quarter inch of the larva. The larva's emergence was not immediate, however, but by the end of the evening, Jerry's maggot had emerged. Oddly, Jerry had grown so attached to his parasite that he had prepared a glass jar with sterilized sand to provide an insect nursery for his pupating larva. Unfortunately, the larva died.[7]

The relationship between Jerry and the maggot is parasitism. Jerry provided food and a home to the parasite to the detriment of the host—himself. In many parasitic relationships, the effects on the host can be much more severe than what Jerry experienced. In Africa, the bite of a blackfly (*Simulium damnosum*) can introduce a parasitic worm that causes a disease referred to as river blindness. The adult parasitic worm produces millions of microscopic parasites that spread throughout the body of its host. In addition to causing blindness, the host experiences skin lesions, disfigurement, and unbearable itching. It is not unusual to see farmers infected with the disease left blind and their mobility reduced to a child leading them around with a stick.

Commensalism and Other Relationships

Commensalism is a relationship between two species where one species benefits and the other is unaffected. It is difficult to prove that a relationship is true commensalism because often the second species will seem unaffected but further investigation shows that there is some effect on the second species. Algae growing on a tree is one example of commensalism where the algae has a place to grow without entering the body of tree.

Hazy distinctions among relationships do exist. The monarch butterfly (*Danaus plexippus*) has a relationship with another butterfly that appears to be commensalism. The brilliantly-colored monarch butterfly feeds on milkweed while it is in the larval stage. Milkweed contains toxic compounds and because the larvae feed on it, the monarch butterfly becomes poisonous to predators who try to eat it. Because of the distinctive black and orange markings on the butterfly, birds learn to avoid the monarch. The viceroy butterfly (*Limenitis archippus*) does not eat the milkweed and is not poisonous. However, the viceroy mimics the coloring of the monarch and incites the same fear in predators and also avoids being eaten. Viceroy butterflies benefit by resembling the monarch and it seems that there is no effect on the monarch by having an impostor in its midst. With further examination, however, in environments where the viceroy is much more common than the monarch, predators might not recognize the black and orange coloration as something to avoid. In an ecological community where predators no longer recognize this coloring as poisonous because the viceroy outnumbers the monarch, the monarch would then be at a disadvantage. The relationship between the monarch and viceroy would then be considered parasitic.

Mutualism is a relationship where both species benefit. It is also referred to as a symbiotic relationship. Species may exchange food or provide shelter, but may be able to both live independently. The Egyptian plover (*Pluvianus aegyptius*) acts as a dentist to crocodiles in sub-Saharan Africa. This blue-gray bird feeds on bits of decaying meat in the crocodiles' teeth. The birds benefit by getting food and the crocodiles benefit by having rotting meat removed from their teeth. Remarkably, the crocodiles do not eat the Egyptian plovers.

2 The Rise of Invasive Terrestrial Animals

●●●●●●●●●●●●

Invasive terrestrial animals are from a foreign environment. They are brought to new environments either intentionally or accidentally and cause harm by displacing native terrestrial animals and altering natural processes. Invasive is not the same thing as being nonnative since many terrestrial animals that are introduced to new environments do not become a nuisance in our environment. Other terms used to refer to these destructive terrestrial animals are invaders, bioinvaders, and exotic species. These terms will be used interchangeably.

THE HUMAN INFLUENCE

Terrestrial animals can walk, fly, or occasionally swim to get around, although reaching another continent is usually a tricky business. People have helped these critters get to much farther reaches than they would on their own. In some cases, terrestrial animals boarded ships and were brought by sailors to new islands; in other situations, insects traveled in soil or plant parts. A hundred or even fifty years ago, there was little worry about moving species around the world. Now we see the potential problems of introducing nonnative species and inadvertently dismantling nature's barriers.

The populations of invasive terrestrial animals increase exponentially each year without any constraints, putting pressure on and altering fragile ecosystems. Valuable species have virtually vanished from America's landscape as a result of these introductions. The elm tree population was nearly decimated as a result of Dutch elm disease.

The cost of controlling these exotic species can be staggering. Insects and plants are sprayed; soil is injected; fields are burned and reseeded; and mammals are trapped at a high annual cost. Eradication becomes impossible and control becomes more costly the longer an invasive species is resident.

People may be the cause of the increase in the number of invasive species but we can also work towards a solution. The first step is to recognize the extent of the problem, (for example, learning how many wild boars live in a particular county or how many snakes have been trapped at Guam's airport.) This kind of information gathering requires the extraordinary coordination of all private and public land management agencies.

Currently, the National Aeronautics and Space Adminstration (NASA) is working with natural resource agencies to determine the extent of invasive plant species using satellite imagery. Another component to solving this problem is for land management agencies to recognize invasive species as a considerable threat to the welfare of the environment and make control one of their priorities. The U.S. Forest Service recognizes the threat of invasive species and limits activities that could be the source of spread such as hay infested with weed seeds. Public agencies such as the Animal and Plant Health Inspection Service (APHIS) of the United States Department of Agriculture (USDA) work to find better ways to control invasive species such as the brown treesnake (*Boiga irregularis*) on the island of Guam. APHIS hires many scientists whose job it is to conduct experiments in the field and lab to find solutions to controlling these invaders.

Regulations are another way to help stop the spread of invasive species. Interstate and international travel of terrestrial animals is regulated by APHIS. APHIS inspects terrestrial animals and plants that are mailed, carried, or shipped into this country by travelers and nursery owners.

APHIS asks every international traveler as they go through customs if they are carrying plant parts in their baggage. Insects could be present on the plant or in plant parts. It only takes the actions of one person to introduce an invasive species that could have devastating impacts on the environment.

APHIS also inspects ports of entry for invasive terrestrial plants and animals. At these inspection stations, inspectors work with specialists in the fields of entomology, botany, and plant pathology to locate, examine, and identify exotic pests, diseases, and noxious weeds. **Entomology** is the study of insects; **botany** is the study of plants; and **plant pathology** is the study of plant disease.

Importers must apply for an agricultural import permit and secure a phytosanitary certificate from the exporting country. Phytosanitary certificates verify that quarantine officials from the exporting country have examined the plants for pests and diseases prior to exporting them. Once the plant arrives in the U.S. port, an inspector examines samples from each species of plant. The inspection process includes a meticulous examination of the leaves, stems, roots, and seeds of the plant.

If an inspector does discover a pest, disease, or noxious weed, they determine the extent of the harm they could cause. Pests that are identified as not existing in the United States or existing to a limited extent, are quarantined, exported, or destroyed.

Like every well-intentioned program, it is not foolproof and occasionally invasive plants or terrestrial animals are accidentally imported. Travelers can do their part by not transporting fruits, plants, seeds, or soil in their baggage.

AWAY FROM HOME WITHOUT THEIR NATURAL ENEMIES

When we were children, we were taught to put things back where they belong. Invasive species are organisms that are not put back where they belong. All organisms have a specific range or habitat. They interact with other organisms that they need and that need them. Moving terrestrial animals around without good reason can create a mess of the environment.

Earthworms in Minnesota are a case of a worm out of place and wreaking havoc. All of the terrestrial earthworms in Minnesota are nonnative. No evidence exists that earthworms ever inhabited Minnesota before European settlement. For the last 11,000 years since the glaciers receded, Minnesota ecosystems developed without earthworms.

The earthworms currently in Minnesota are originally from Europe and Asia, and arrived in contaminated soil on ships. It may seem odd to indicate that earthworms could be a problem anywhere considering their virtue of turning waste into fertile soil. But it is all a matter of the earthworm being in an environment where it did not evolve.

The nonnative earthworms in Minnesota are eating the precious decaying fallen leaves that the hardwood forest needs to thrive. Minnesota's hardwood forests developed in the absence of earthworms. Without earthworms, fallen leaves decompose slowly, creating a spongy layer of organic material.[8] This layer of organic material is necessary for the growth of Minnesota's native vegetation. The sponginess of this layer also provides habitat for ground-dwelling woodland terrestrial animals and prevents soil erosion. These nonnative worms eat this much-needed organic matter in some places until there is none left. This situation is particularly devastating for young seedlings, ferns, and wildflowers that rely on this organic matter more than do the mature trees. In places where wooded areas have been heavily invaded by these nonnative earthworms, nutrients leach out of the soil. This along with soil erosion muddies adjacent streams and degrades fish habitat.

Another problem with invasive terrestrial animals is that they generally do not have predators in their new environments. In their native region, invasive terrestrial animals are kept in control by natural predators. Natural predators include other animals and pathogens (diseases). As these invaders found their way into our environment, the organisms that keep their populations in control were left behind. Natural predators are crucial to nature's balance of predator and prey.

PREDATOR-PREY RELATIONSHIPS

Predator-prey relationships are the interactions where one species is a food source or prey for the other species. A predator is an animal that eats other animals. The prey is the animal that the predator is eating. Predators and prey in action have been depicted on nature shows on television where the cheetah runs down the gazelle and eats it. Insects and plants also have predator-prey relationships. Animals rely on many organisms, just as many organisms rely on their presence; the predator-prey relationship is just one type of interaction. Interactions among living things and their environment are often referred to as "the web of life."

Predators and prey evolve together and occur naturally in the environment. The predator encourages the fittest of the prey species. Prey will try to avoid being eaten and will therefore develop characteristics to prevent death. The prey may evolve to be faster if the predator is a chasing animal. The prey may also develop a better sense of smell, sight, or camouflage. Characteristics that the prey possesses that do not enable them to escape the predator would not be improved or refined. Similarly, characteristics that predators have that enable them to catch their prey, like claws, sharp teeth, and keen eyesight, would be developed over time.

Predator-prey relationships are nature's way of keeping species in balance. The predator's population may be larger than usual one season but will decrease because of the limits on food (the prey). Separating the predator from its prey knocks the system out of balance and causes a potentially damaging situation for the environment—a "superspecies" may emerge for which there are few controls on the population.

Insects and Fire

Insects are predators to trees. Insect damage is considered a natural disturbance in a healthy, functioning ecosystem. Fire and wind damage are other disturbances that a healthy forest will be able to deal with. This natural relationship can get out of whack when the predation on trees by an exotic (invasive) insect with an out-of-control population growth takes a toll on the living forest. Not only will there be more dead trees in the forest, there will be a greater chance of fire because of all the deadwood.

The Lesson of the Cane Toad

Biological control is the method of introducing an invasive species' natural predator as a means to keep the invasive species under control. The concern is that the introduced species may itself become a pest. Early on in the days of biological control, these mistakes were made. Now, introduced species undergo lengthy experiments by federal agencies to make sure they will not adversely affect native species.

The cane toad (*Bufo marinus*) was introduced worldwide to biologically control pests of sugarcane (Figure 2.1). True, the cane toad did eat pests of sugarcane, but it ended up eating just about anything else in its path. In addition to the loss of the

Figure 2.1 The cane toad was originally introduced as a biological method for controlling pests of sugarcane. Instead, the cane toad now is a pest itself. Scientists now examine the potential effects of biological control agents before they are introduced into a new environment.

organisms that it ate, this toad displaced native amphibians by competing for food and breeding habitat.

The cane toad's native habitat is subtropical rain forests, but it will also live almost anywhere including man-made ponds, gardens, drain pipes, debris, and cement piles. This toad prefers dry ground but can tolerate high levels of salinity.

The cane toad secretes toxic compounds from its glands when it is provoked, particularly when a predator grasps the toad in its mouth. Anecdotal accounts from Australia recount stories of pythons found dead with the toad in its mouth or guts. The toxic secretions from the toad have also caused illness and death to domestic animals. Cane toads can squirt the toxic secretions more than 3 feet (.9 meter) to protect themselves. Even humans have died from eating the cane toad eggs or the cane toad itself.

Cane toads are voracious eaters. They primarily eat arthropods but will consume anything they can catch. Cane toads have been reported eating rotting garbage, fledgling birds, and even a lit cigarette butt. If these toads had consumed only the pests that they were intended to feed on, it would have been an immensely successful biological control campaign. However, because these toads are not host-specific, there has been a decline in native species such as lizards and other amphibians. A **host-specific** organism will typically consume only one species.

The Benefits of the Cane Toad

If invasive species could be harvested and sold or used, some say they would no longer be invasive because humans would be their natural predator. In the case of the cane toad, this does occur to a limited extent.

In Australia, *Pete's Bizarre Bazaar* sells cane toad leather products. Pete boasts of some of the most unusual gift items such as toad hatbands, purses, hats, and cigarette lighter cases all resembling the toad in some form. Pete's Web site mentions that the leather comes from Australia's eradication program where the toads are humanely killed. In addition to being used to create accessories, the cane toad is also the amphibian of choice for dissections in high school biology classes. The venom from the cane toad is believed to have pharmacological benefits for use in heart disease drugs.

Unfortunately, the cane toad still is a little too underexploited for its spread to be stabilized. The number of cane toads present in Queensland, Australia, has been described as plaguelike.

Australia has millions of cane toads and its range appears to be expanding. The cane toads disperse by hitching on Australian freight trucks. The toads get inside the truck and are hidden within the cargo. The cane toad has done well in Australia because there are no natural predators to keep them under control and there is an ample supply of small vertebrates and invertebrates for them to eat.

FROM DOMESTIC TO FERAL

A domesticated animal that lives outside fending for itself will have an altered behavior that threatens people and the environment. A lap cat that snuggles with its owner and meows gently for more, purring when it finds a sunny spot by the

Insects and Chemistry: Infochemicals

A corn earworm caterpillar (*Helicoverpa zea*) is eating a cotton leaf plant. The caterpillar drools just a bit, alerting the plant to the presence of volicitin, which is only found in insect's oral secretions. The cotton plant releases a blend of volatile compounds. This signature scent is recognized by a parasitic insect indicating the presence of a caterpillar. The parasitic insect responds by depositing her eggs within the caterpillar. The larvae eventually eat the caterpillar. Both plant and the parasitic insect benefit from this interaction. As mentioned, a relationship where both species benefit is called a mutualistic relationship.

The chemical compounds released by the plant are called terpenes. Smell a rose. Its fragrance is due to the volatility of terpenes. Parasitic insects find their food through terpene cues. Plants defend themselves based on their ability to produce terpenes. A clever strategy, given that the plant must create a defense system while staying rooted in the same location.

window can become a fearsome predator of songbirds if cast outside by a careless owner. A previously domesticated animal that is living life on its own is referred to as **feral**. Feral animals are considered invasive; they did not evolve with the environment they currently live in and they usually cause damage. They compete with native animals for food and shelter; they destroy habitat and often prey on native animals. Feral animals generally have few natural predators and often have high reproductive rates; therefore their populations rapidly multiply.

The ecology of Australia has suffered from feral animals such as the rabbit. In 1859, a mere 20 rabbits were released into the wild. By the 1950s, rabbits had reached plague proportions and today they are one of the most destructive animals in Australia.

Insects also use volatile compounds to find the best place to lay their eggs. Female parasitic wasps must find a host, such as a caterpillar, to inject their eggs. This process paralyzes the caterpillar while the larvae grow in and feed on the host.

Compounds such as these are infochemicals. Pheromones are a particular type of infochemical released within species for reproductive purposes. Next time a mosquito lands on your windshield or window, look to see if it is male or female. A male has tiny hairs on his antennae. These hairlike structures catch the molecules of the pheromones of the female. Insects also use infochemicals to find food, mates, and sites for their eggs and young.

These infochemicals are responsible for the interactions among plants, herbivore insects, and predatory insects. If left to chance, a wasp could spend her entire life searching for a host. Without infochemicals, many predatory insects would not survive.

The rabbits consume large amounts of precious vegetation and erode the soil by digging burrows.

Feral animals will often breed with domestic animals, compounding the problem of controlling their populations. The wild boar that was introduced from Europe for sport hunting escaped its enclosures and began to interbreed with domestic pigs, which resulted in hybrid wild hogs.

The Red Imported Fire Ant

MARCHING ACROSS THE SOUTH

3

• •

After World War II, soldiers returned to the United States and eagerly bought newly constructed homes to start their new life. A housing boom began and along with the newly built homes, sod and nursery plants were transported across the American landscape. And so began the invasion of fire ants across the South.

The ants traveled in the soil of the landscaping plants. In 1953, the United States Department of Agriculture (USDA) recognized the link between the landscaping plants and the imported fire ant and assigned $2.4 million for control and eradication. Time and again, invasive species prove to be exceedingly difficult to control once they have become well established.

The red imported fire ant is a much more aggressive species than the black imported fire ant and has spread throughout the southern United States and Puerto Rico. The red fire ant is so aggressive that it has actually displaced the black imported fire ant in some places. Of more concern is the displacement of ecologically important species such as birds, reptiles, and insects by these invasive ants.

HOW THE FIRE ANTS ARRIVED

The black imported fire ant (*Solenopsis richteri*) and the red imported fire ant (*Solenopsis invicta*) both arrived in the early

1900s, probably from soil used as ballast in cargo ships (Figure 3.1). **Ballast** is the material that the ships use to maintain stability during transit. When a ship is empty of cargo, it sits high in the water and can be more easily overturned by wind or waves. To make travel safer, the ship fills its tank with something that has weight, such as soil. When cargo is put on the ship,

Figure 3.1 Ballast contained in cargo ships is a significant method of transporting invasive species to new environments. A ship's ballast weighs it down, but often this ballast contains plants and animals that will thrive without predators in other regions.

the ballast material is no longer needed and it is dumped, whereby nonnative organisms are introduced into a foreign environment.

Today, fire ants continue to spread throughout the United States through mating flights, colony movement, transport of contaminated soil, or even rafting during flooding. Although originally introduced into the South, the imported fire ant has been found as far west as California and as far north as Maryland and Kansas.

The Imported Fire Ant's Life Cycle

The imported fire ant experiences four different stages before its life is over (unless a predator gets to it sooner). Those stages are egg, larva, pupa, and adult. The egg, larval, and pupal stages occur within the underground nest and are only seen when the nests are disturbed or when they are being carried to a different location by workers. The eggs are nearly microscopic. The workers feed the larvae and once the larvae mature, they **molt** into pupae. Molting is the process of shedding an exterior coating to reveal new growth. Insects have hormones that initiate the molt.

The pupae look like adults except that their legs and antennae are held tightly against their body. The pupae are white but darken as they mature. The pupa matures and then molts into an adult.

Most of the ants become sterile worker ants, all of them female and wingless. Ants that are fertile must get more food during their development; they are also larger than the sterile workers. These larger, fertile ants are future queens and have wings. The males also have wings but have a smaller head.

Sex occurs in the air. During this mating flight the fertile females and males mate in the air before falling back to the ground. The males then die; the females remove their own wings, dig a hole in the soil, and seal themselves in the ground where they will lay their eggs. These eggs will hatch and become worker ants. Some fire ant colonies only have one queen, whereas others have many. Colonies with many queens are much more difficult to control because all of the queens must be killed to prevent the colony from surviving.[9]

Agricultural and Ecosystem Influences

Like all native animals, ants play an important role in the ecological balance. They are part of the food chain, providing food for other animals. They also help break down wood and other plant materials in the process of decomposition, which enriches the soil.

The imported fire ants feed on insects as well as plants. They attack saplings and seedlings. Fire ants damage 57 species of agricultural plants. In addition, they feed on the germinating seeds and buds of crop plants as well as developing fruits. The tunneling behavior of these ants has been particularly damaging to crops that grow underground, such as potatoes. By eating the buds of plants, the ant prevents the plant from flowering and the subsequent pollination by insects. Fire ants are even able to destroy the bark of trees such as citrus and pecan. If the bark is cut all the way around—known as girdling—the tree will die because it cannot get water to the upper parts of the tree. The bark transports nutrients and water.

Fire ants are particularly devastating to ground-nesting animals including reptiles, birds, and mammals. Populations of field mice, turtles, and snakes have seen their populations reduced when fire ants have been able to take hold in their ecosystem.

Imported fire ants are notorious for their mounds (Figure 3.2). The cone-shaped dome resembles a large gopher mound. It is made of soil and has a hard, rain-resistant crust. These mounds

Figure 3.2 Imported fire ants are notorious for their mounds, which are often mistaken for gopher mounds. These mounds help keep ants warm and dry underground.

have no external openings. Well below the top of the mound, worker ants are slaving away in the tunnels. The mound has three functions: 1) it serves as a flight platform for nuptial flights; 2) it raises the colony above the water table in saturated ground; and 3) it acts as a passive solar collector to supply warmth to the colony during the cold winter months.[10] But the survival of this ant species does not require the creation of the mound; rotted logs, walls of buildings, automobiles, sidewalks, and dried cow manure can all serve as home to the imported fire ant.

Human Interaction with the Fire Ant

After Hurricane Katrina hit the Gulf Coast in 2005, a man was forced up into a tree by the flooding below. He couldn't

Ant Hills: A True Matriarchy

It pays to be female and fertile if you're an ant. Ant nests usually have a queen whose only job it is to mate and lay eggs. Whereas the human working female only gets a few weeks or months off of work after giving birth, the queen never has to work again. . . . or take care of her young! In the case of the fire ants, the sterile, female workers find food and take care of the young. Males serve the simple role of mating and then die afterwards.

Argentine ants, also a nonnative, invasive species, have usually 10 to 20 queens with some nests having as many as 100 queens in the community with approximately 35,000 workers. Argentine ants were introduced through Brazilian coffee shipments to the New Orleans port. In this matriarchy, warfare between neighboring Argentine colonies does not exist, rather the queens opt to join nests together through a network of tunnels. Clearly this is a system that works well for the spreading Argentine ants, much to the dismay of homeowners.

swim. With both hands around the tree, fire ants ravaged his face, creating pustules that would eventually lead to scarring.

The imported fire ant possesses a mandible (jaw) that delivers a bite and a stinger that punishes its disturber with a painful sting. It stings in response to any disturbance of the colony or their food source. Each ant will repeatedly sting even after their venom sac has been depleted. Some people are hypersensitive to the venom and may have reactions such as dizziness, nausea, chest pains, shock or, in some cases, coma.

Repeated stings can disfigure human skin. A white pustule forms about a day or two after a person has been stung (Figure 3.3). The pustule must be kept clean or else it can become infected. If infection occurs, a person could be left with permanent scarring.

Populations of fire ants can ruin parks and picnic areas because people are afraid of the ants. Fire ants are attracted by electrical currents and cause damage to heat pumps, air conditioners, telephone junction boxes, transformers, traffic lights, and gasoline pumps. Traffic accidents have been caused by drivers being stung while driving. As a double whammy, accident victims who have been thrown from their cars can then be attacked by fire ants.

NATIVE FIRE ANTS

Native fire ants exist in several southern states, including Texas and Florida. When in their native environment, these fire ants do not pose a problem.

The best way to distinguish red imported fire ants from other ant species is their aggressive nature when their colony is disturbed. The gopher-like mounds are also specific to the imported fire ants. Other ant species sting, but the sting of the native fire ant does not produce a pustule; therefore, the native

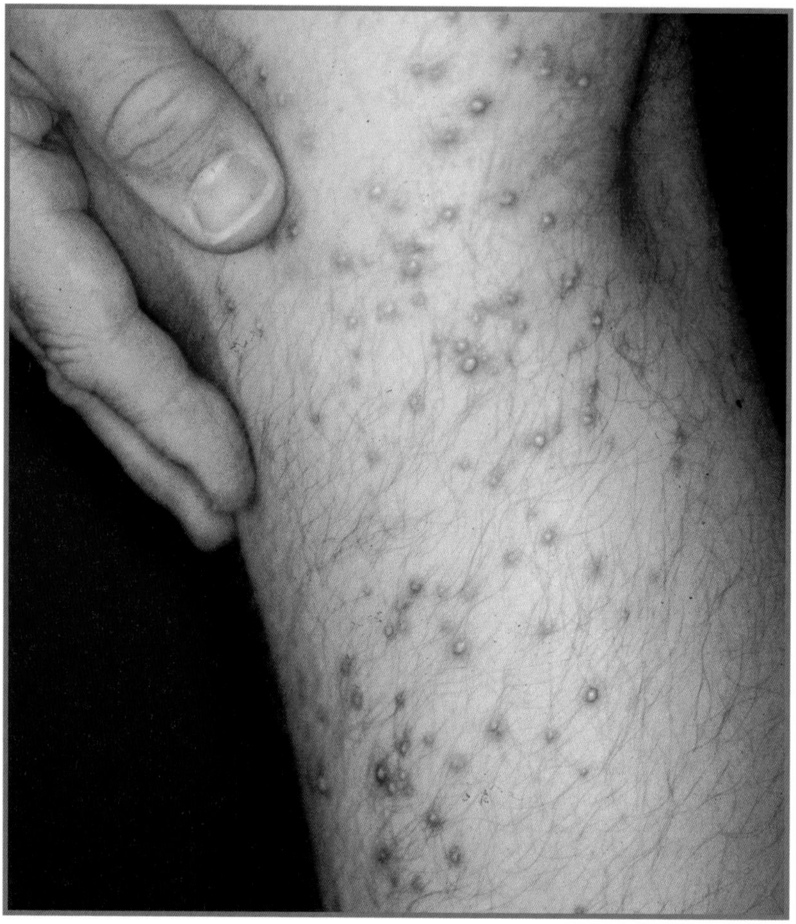

Figure 3.3 The imported fire ant delivers a painful sting when the mound is disturbed. With a powerful jaw, the ant will continue to sting even when the venom sac is depleted. Pustules such as these develop within a couple of days after the stinging.

ant's sting may be painful but at least secondary infection or scarring does not occur.

IMPORTED FIRE ANT CONTROL

Most people can manage to live with ants even though they are a nuisance. Some ants, such as carpenter ants, simply need to be restricted from entering the home. Imported fire ants are far too aggressive to tolerate in the home or even the yard. In many southern states, controlling imported fire ants over a large area is impractical, yet control strategies on specific areas do yield results. California, luckily, is still able to focus on eradication and encourages homeowners not to attempt to control the ants on their own, but to instead call the U.S. Department of Food and Agriculture.

Killing the Queen

The queen rules in the imported fire ant community. To wipe out a colony, the queen must be killed. To be certain of this, mounds must be treated with precision. Targeting individual mounds is a labor-intensive, yet effective method of imported fire ant control. It is important to prevent disturbance; otherwise, the person initiating the control could be in for a nasty surprise. The mound is soaked with a common insecticide. One problem with this method is that often the queen is buried too deeply in the mound to be killed. As an alternative, the insecticide can be injected deep into the mound to increase the chance that the queen is killed. It is crucial to kill the queen in these colonies or else she will mate, reproduce, and the community will quickly rebound.

Baiting the Workers

Broadcast insecticide treatments focus on a larger area and are less specific. Unfortunately, the insecticide used is not specific to imported fire ants and the poison can kill other valuable insects. Bait can be a piece of ant food, such as corn, injected with poison. The foraging workers will take the poisoned food back to the colony and unknowingly feed it to the other members. The advantage of using bait is that one does not have to spend time finding a mound to use it. The cost on a per-acre basis is also much less expensive than mound treatments. However, bait may also readily dissolve in contact with water, so an unexpected rain could wipe out any control endeavors.

Propagating the Protozoa

One of the fire ant's natural enemies is a protozoan disease, *Thelohania solenopsae.* A protozoa is a microscopic organism similar to an amoeba. Using a protozoa to control the imported fire ant is biological control, whereas mound treatments and baits are chemical control methods.

This South American protozoa infects the colony and debilitates the queen and about 25% of the workers. It has yet to be introduced as a biological control to the United States as there is concern about the effect on native ants: harvester, carpenter, and leaf-cutting. Currently, the protozoa are grown in labs so that they will not escape until the effect on native ants can be determined.

Two other South American species are being evaluated as possible biological control agents: Phorid flies (*Pseudaceton spp.*) and an ant called a workerless social parasite (*Solenopsis dagerrei*).

Phorid flies deposit their eggs on the worker fire ants outside the mound. When the fly maggots emerge from the eggs, they feed on the ant's head. As imagined, this becomes quite a problem for the ant and eventually leads to decapitation. Over the years, the fire ants have caught on and the workers will not go out to forage. The colony then has a difficult time feeding itself since it relies on the foraging of its workers. This fly controls the imported fire ants' access to food and therefore enables other native ant species to compete more fairly.

The workerless social parasite ant attaches to the fire ant queen and manipulates the fire ant workers to babysit the parasite's own young to the disregard of the workers' baby ants.

There is no worker caste in the parasite's community; only queens and males are produced. This ant has a debilitating effect on the fire ant colony and the number of sexual ants produced in the colony. Eventually, the fire ant colony will collapse.

All of these potential biological control agents offer a long-range, chemical-free alternative to insecticides. However, not enough is known about them at present to use them. Extensive research must be conducted to evaluate their success and make sure that they, in turn, do not become a pest.

The Brown Treesnake

EATING GUAM'S BIRDS
TO EXTINCTION

• • • • • • • • • • • • • •

Day approaches dusk as a cargo ship full of petroleum products gets ready to leave Apra Harbor in Guam. The cargo is headed for Hawaii. Roughly three times the size of Washington, D.C., Guam is the United States' westernmost territory. Apra Harbor faces the Philippine Sea and is plentiful with coral reefs.

The port inspector wipes his brow as the tropical weather has yet to be cooled by an afternoon shower. Using his foot to push aside an empty box, the inspector pokes a stick behind a barrel. An eight-foot long snake quickly raises the front of its body in a striking position. This nocturnal snake was sleeping. The inspector knows that no one has died of a bite from the brown treesnake, but he knows many people that have gone to the hospital as a result of it. The snake is aggressive and flattens its head to appear larger. The inspector takes a step forward and the snake lunges to bite him. The inspector is familiar with the brown treesnake, having grown up on this island. The inspector uses a hook to grab the snake and put it in a burlap sack. The snake will later be placed in alcohol to be positively identified. Over the five-year period from 1994 to 1998, approximately 5,400 brown treesnakes were captured in Guam's civilian airport facility.

The brown treesnake likes to hide itself in small spaces during the day while it sleeps. It was this trait that likely led to its accidental shipment in military cargo to Guam after World War II.

Threatened and Endangered Species: Who Protects Them?

According to the great biologist E.O. Wilson, invasive species are the second leading cause of species endangerment; the first is habitat loss. Given this, many organizations that work to protect native species from extinction also recognize the importance of controlling invasive species.

The Nature Conservancy is one such agency. Whereas the group's members once feared the bulldozer and cement truck, now they are more concerned about the silent spread of invasive species. The Nature Conservancy is an example of a private, nonprofit organization that raises money to purchase land and then protects and manages the land and wildlife. Federal, state, and local government groups also are responsible for protecting endangered species. The Wildlife Services (WS) program within APHIS is responsible for guarding against invasive species as well as protecting threatened and endangered species.

Wildlife Services plays a crucial role in wolf reintroduction programs in the western United States. As new wolf populations become established, WS works to prevent livestock predation by wolves and relocate problem animals. Wildlife Services works with landowners frustrated by the presence of wolves that eat their livestock. Because of these cooperative efforts between landowners and agencies, the wolf has been successfully reintroduced into Yellowstone National Park. Protecting endangered species employs elements of invasive species management, habitat protection, and communication with the public.

If this snake had the same disposition as a rattlesnake, it would have been a less likely hitchhiker. A rattlesnake may appear to be much more threatening to humans, but the brown treesnake presents a true danger to Guam's economy and ecology.

THE BROWN TREESNAKE'S EFFECTS ON NATIVE WILDLIFE

Nature has devised its own method of protecting islands from interloper species—large bodies of water. Animals such as snakes and large reptiles are unable to cross oceans and are naturally absent from islands. Humans started using planes and boats and inadvertently broke down these natural barriers. Animals that reach oceanic islands develop island tameness, which is a lack of fear of humans and other predators. On more than one occasion, people have brought species to Guam with disastrous results to native species; the brown treesnake is just one example.

As with nearly all invasive species, the problem is a lack of natural predators. The brown treesnake (*Boiga irreguleris*) is native from eastern Indonesia to the Solomon Islands and northern Australia (Figure 4.1). This snake has a liking for trees and as a result, it has caused 9 out of 12 of Guam's forest birds to go extinct, half of its lizards, and probably some of its bats. Guam's native wildlife evolved without snakes or other stealthy, nocturnal, arboreal predators, and therefore does not know to fear them. This fact, coupled with the abundance of small prey, enabled the brown treesnake to explode in population.

According to the USGS, nearly all species of Guam's native wildlife have suffered, including reptiles, birds, and mammals (Figure 4.2). The snake uses its venom to subdue and kill its prey before eating it. The snake usually wraps its body around the prey to immobilize it while chewing to inject the venom.

Figure 4.1 The brown treesnake is a hungry predator of Guam's wildlife. Vigilant efforts must be made to prevent this snake from hiding in cargo and being inadvertently transported to new locations.

Islands are more vulnerable to introduced predators. Islands tend to have less biodiversity and are more easily affected by changes in the ecosystem. It has been stated that the impact of invader species such as the brown treesnake on islands has caused more ecological devastation than the naval bombardment and leveling of forests that occurred on Guam during World War II. The war wiped out large tracts of land that were able to recover once the fighting ended. But once an introduced species has eliminated a native species, time can offer no chance for recovery.[11]

THE BROWN TREESNAKE'S EFFECTS ON THE ECONOMY

Guam has a power outage on average every three days due to the brown treesnake. The snakes cross power lines, simultaneously

Figure 4.2 Populations of rare birds such as this Micronesian king-fisher are dwindling from the predations of the brown treesnake. The brown treesnake wraps itself around its prey and then injects its venom into it, giving its unsuspecting victim little hope of escape.

contact charged conductors and grounded objects, and short out the circuits. Outages cause food spoilage and computer failures. By almost anybody's standards, this is a difficult way to run a country.

Guam relies heavily on tourism for revenue. Brown treesnakes can reach lengths of 11 feet (3.3 meters) and can startle tourists to the extent that they will no longer want to visit. For example, the Tree Bar is a poolside bar in one of Guam's largest hotels. The bar was forced to cut down a large fig tree by the bar because of the abundance of brown treesnakes that would dangle from the branches and scare vacationers. Invasion of these snakes into homes decreases property values and the general enjoyment of life on the island. This snake also crawls into poultry houses and yards to consume domestic poultry, eggs, pet birds, and other small pets.

THE BROWN TREESNAKE'S EFFECTS ON HUMANS

The brown treesnake's bite is not as deadly as a rattlesnake, but it does inject a weak venom. The brown treesnake lacks fangs and therefore must chew its target; the weak venom is conducted by the enlarged rear teeth. Obviously, human adults will not allow the snake to chew, but defenseless infants have been victims. No deaths have occurred but some infants have suffered respiratory arrest due to the venom. Luckily, medical treatment was readily available to prevent a fatality.

BROWN TREESNAKE CONTROL

People's reactions to the brown treesnake's effect on Guam's native animals, ecology, and economy span a range of opinions: "Why don't you just get rid of the snake?" or…"Surely, now that everything is gone the snake has run out of food and will die off on its own."[12] Unfortunately, the situation is not that simple. The problem with the snakes is now so big that getting rid of them is impossible using existing and even developing technologies.

One method is through trapping and conducting night searches at port facilities, specifically of outbound cargo and vehicles in Guam. Much of this cargo is bound for Hawaii. Dogs are used to sniff out these snakes. In Hawaii, incoming cargo and planes are inspected by the Hawaii Department of Agriculture. In addition, staff from the Hawaii Department of Land and Natural Resources are trained to identify the brown treesnake. No snakes are native to Hawaii although the small, harmless blind snake (*Ramphotyphlops braminus*) has become established.

The difficulty in controlling the brown treesnake is that control methods do not completely work. Small snakes are able to elude traps. Another problem is that the snakes move around during the day. This makes it difficult to set traps where snakes have been seen, hoping that they will return to that location. A combination of methods has the best chance of success.

The traps used for brown treesnakes have a funnel design, similar to ones used in commercial minnow or crayfish traps; the treesnake traps are used around forested plots, fences, buildings, and other sites. A mouse cage containing a live mouse will attract the snake. A dead mouse would be just as effective but decay occurs quickly in Guam's tropical environment. The snake is generally not interested in the mouse two to three days after it has died. Putting a live mouse in each trap is quite costly. Scientists are examining the use of mouse odors rather than live mice to attract the snakes. Presently, substances as diverse as tofu, plaster of paris, and gelatin have shown promise as attractive lures, but snakes have shown only limited interest. Another idea is to inject a live mouse with a chemical that would make the snake sterile.

Much thought goes into where to place the traps and how many to place within a given space. Once snake populations have been reduced in an area, maintaining some strategically placed traps around the plot helps deter population recovery.

Toxicants are an additional way to control the brown treesnake. Toxicants are any substance that can cause death, disease, injury, or birth defects when ingested. A fumigant is a toxicant that is applied as a gas. A fumigant is best used on outbound cargo to kill the snakes. This control technique ensures that the snake does not reach other countries.

Acetaminophen, the main ingredient in many over-the-counter pain relievers, is poisonous to the brown treesnakes even at low levels. Since the snake is unlikely to swallow a pill, dead mice could be injected with acetaminophen. The snake would then eat the mouse. Thousands of hours of video monitoring revealed that other desirable species do not eat or at least are not affected by the presence of acetaminophen-injected dead mice.

There is considerable concern that this snake may spread to Hawaii, where invasive species are already a significant problem. Because the climates of Hawaii and Guam are similar, it is feared that the same devastation could occur to Hawaii's ecosystems if this snake is able to make its way there. Several state and federal agencies have been working together to make sure that this does not happen.

5

The Wild Boar

PIGGING OUT IN AMERICAN FIELDS AND FORESTS

• • • • • • • • • • • • • • • • • • • •

In Tennessee, the ancient sport of boar hunting has been revived. It is fall in Cherokee National Forest and hunters are preparing for the annual hunt of what is locally called the "Rooshian" wild hog. Wild boars have been given this nickname because it is believed that they were imported by Russian sportsmen. Hunters are chosen from a lottery system by the state game and fish division as well as the U.S. Forest Service. Hunters often use dogs to chase the boar within shooting distance. The chase of dogs, hunter, and boar can last for miles. Some dogs end up shredded to ribbons by the razor-sharp tusks of a cornered boar.

Wild boars (*Sus scrofa*), also known as wild pigs, wild hogs, European wild boars, Russian wild boars, and razorbacks, look similar to the domestic pig yet are aggressive mammals that pose a serious economic, health, and ecological threat (Figure 5.1). Wild boars usually weigh between 110 and 130 pounds and have elongated, flattened snouts with long, uncoiled tails. Adults develop a thick, scruffy mane with stiff bristles tipped blond, hence the alternate name of razorback. They also have four continually growing tusks that can be painfully sharp; they use their tusks for defense and to establish dominance during mating.

Florida received the first introduced wild boar as early as the 1500s. In 1893, 50 feral pigs from Germany's Black Forest were released on a hunting preserve in New Hampshire's Blue

Figure 5.1 Wild boars were introduced from Europe for sport hunting. The wild boars escaped their confined locations and began to breed with domestic pigs. These boars roam 10 miles (6 kilometers) daily in search of food and cause damage to habitat and crops in the process.

Mountains. A few years later, Russian wild boars were released in North Carolina on a preserve and more were released on Santa Cruz Island in California. At that time, no one believed that the wild boars would escape the preserves, possibly breed with other pigs, and pose a problem. Today, feral pigs are found in at least 23 states. Biologists estimate the feral pig population to be approximately four million.

WILD BOAR BIOLOGY AND BEHAVIOR

The wild boar roams an area of roughly 10 miles, but if food is in short supply, the boar may roam up to 50 square miles using its strong sense of smell to sniff out roots, tubers, and small animals. Boars hear well but don't see well, choosing to communicate by grunting and squealing though they are generally solitary creatures. Despite their stocky appearance, boars can run up to 30 miles per hour and are good swimmers. They prefer to nest and rest in dense vegetation and secluded thickets. They generally inhabit swamps, brushlands, woodlands near agricultural fields, and forests.

Wild boars are rapid breeders. A boar will reach sexual maturity at one year of age and have litters of three to eight piglets. Females are pregnant for approximately four months.

Natural predators of adult boars are humans, bears, wolves, and panthers. Piglets are taken by bobcats, coyotes, and other

Hawaii and Invasives: Too Many Unwanted Visitors

The first wild pigs were brought to the Hawaiian Islands by Polynesians nearly 1,500 years ago. The pigs became feral and spread with an appetite for certain plants into grasslands, woodlands, and forests.

Before human introduction of species, mammals were few in Hawaii. The only native mammals are the bat and seal. Seals and bats, however, aren't nearly as damaging to the plant communities. The pig is highly adaptive and its behavior consists of rooting, rutting, digging, and degrading until fragile, native species that have not evolved mechanisms to deal with these aggressions are displaced.

Pigs are just one of the many invasive species in Hawaii. Islands are particularly vulnerable to exotic invasions because native species haven't evolved to the same extent as their counterparts medium-sized carnivores such as raccoons. Larger boars will cannibalize the smaller ones.

Wild boars are omnivores that will eat almost anything in their path, yet preferring acorns, hickory, and beechnuts in the autumn. At other times of the year they eat plants, agricultural crops, insects, crayfish, frogs, salamanders, snakes, mice, eggs of ground-nesting birds, young rabbits, fawns, and young livestock such as lambs, calves, and kids. In addition to the destruction that they do by trampling and rooting up vegetation for food, they will scratch and dig in wet ground to create depressions or wallows to roll around in and to escape heat and insects during

in continental ecosystems. There are fewer individuals to breed and interact with; essentially, the native species on an island are less fit. If species are less fit, they will have a more difficult time competing with invasive species.

Island ecosystems are generally smaller in land area and therefore less biologically rich than large ones. Perhaps another reason why Hawaii has so many invasive species is due to the number of tourists who may inadvertently bring seeds attached to their clothing. Whatever the reason may be, invasive species push many of Hawaii's native species to extinction. Twenty-five percent of all endangered plants and birds are in Hawaii. Six endangered bird species seek refuge in Hawaii Volcanoes National Park; they depend directly on the remaining portions of native habitat now under siege by invasive species.

the hot, insect-infested months. The damage they cause in moist soils is much more severe than in dry soils. Removal of the vegetation can also cause significant erosion.

In wooded areas, the wild boar reduces the leaf litter because of its appetite. Some animals rely on this leaf litter and even if the wild boar does not eat them, these animals will leave wild boar habitat. The red-backed vole and short-tailed shrew that are found in the Great Smoky Mountains National Park rely on this leaf litter. Places where the wild boar has intensively rooted have virtually no red-backed voles or short-tailed shrews.

In addition to damaging vegetation and crops, wild boars compete with native white-tailed deer and also cause population declines of quail and wild turkey populations in other states. The wallows they create muddy the waters of wetlands and ponds, destroy aquatic vegetation, and reduce water quality. Because wetlands are generally more biologically rich than other ecosystems, the wild boar's damage has far-reaching effects.

WILD BOAR MANAGEMENT

The removal of wild boars is crucial to the protection of many terrestrial and wetland habitats. Many natural resource agencies promote aggressive removal of these boars. In Wisconsin, there is no closed season or harvest limit on the animals. Wisconsin landowners are not required to have a hunting permit if they are shooting boars on their own property.

In the Great Smoky Mountains National Park (GSMNP), boars are a considerable concern in this vast, protected area. The wild boar was released in the early 1900s as part of a business venture in the mountains of North Carolina, near the area that is now the park. The boars escaped their enclosures and were able to proliferate in the mountains for nearly a decade.

In the 1950s, control efforts resulted in the annual killing of approximately 60 wild boars. Currently, 300 wild boars are

Reestablish the Wild Boar?

In Britain, the Mammal Society is working to reestablish the wild boar. Yes, this is the same wild boar that the United States is trying to get rid of. How can it be that one continent is feverishly trying to get rid of an animal they find so destructive and yet another continent is forlornly missing it? It all comes down to what belongs where. The boar is native to Britain and probably became extinct there at the end of the thirteenth century. While it is true that the boar has a face only a mother boar could love, Britain's Mammal Society wants to reestablish all native mammals that have gone extinct.

Boars will still root just as they do in the United States and the Society has expressed concern over the welfare of some of its more precious vegetation, but Britain does not see the same level of destruction as occurs in places such as the Great Smoky Mountains. Their goal is the reintroduction of pure boars—none of those that are hybrids with domestic pigs. Stories of wild boar populations excite the Society but they insist on genetic testing to make sure it is a pure wild boar breed. According to the Society, little conservation interest would be attached to a population of feral domestic pig crosses.

removed from the park annually. This is not sufficient to prevent harm to the park's ecosystem from the boar's rooting behavior. Part of the problem was that wild boars were being killed only in the more easily accessible areas of the park such as paved areas and locations near hog hunting shelters and the Appalachian Trail.

Land managers decided to retrieve 26 years of wild boar removal records and review the data geographically. Some of the data were already referenced with latitude and longitude. The rest of the boar removals were marked on a map and each point was given latitude and longitude readings. After the data was displayed on the map, it was clear that boar removal was not uniform throughout the park but actually was clustered. Clustered killing of wild boars was found to be a less effective strategy. Managers decided the best success would be more consistent removal efforts. The control officers in the park used global positioning system (GPS) receivers to more accurately record where a boar was killed. The initiative was to track the boar removals and make sure the removal is more consistent throughout the park.

Using GPS Technology

Using satellites already in space, we can use equipment to figure out where we are on the Earth. The location is recorded in latitude and longitude along with the time. It is easy to understand why this type of technology can be so helpful in managing natural resources. Envision the vastness of a national park; trying to pinpoint an exact location relying solely on memory would be impossible. Even with a topographic map, estimations would be rough. Using technology that pinpoints locations is a tremendous tool for natural resource managers trying to track animals or plants. Global positioning system (GPS) units are the hardware that is used out in the field. GPS data usually entails a mountable or handheld device that records the place on Earth where the person holding it is located. This equipment is then plugged into a computer and the information is downloaded. GPS data alone is marginally useful, but combined with other geographic information, such as that used to make maps, such data can be extraordinarily useful in creating management plans.

The GPS data is integrated with another data layer, such as a map, to show the location of the GPS point. GPS units are popular with hikers because the GPS unit has a screen that retains the data and can direct a person in case they get separated from the trail.

6 The European Starling
BLAME IT ON SHAKESPEARE

• •

At the Peace Valley Nature Center in Doylestown, Pennsylvania, birds are the reason a group of dedicated individuals gets up at 6 A.M. every Saturday, rain or shine. The Peace Valley Nature Center is wooded habitat with streams and ponds, usually teeming with birds in the early morning hours. A flurry in the trees causes the group to eagerly lift their binoculars to their eyes. Disappointed, it was just another starling. One man mumbles "trash bird" under his breath. As the morning moves on, they come across a tree with what looks like 400 starlings in it and not a native bird in sight.

WHO DID IT?

In 1890, a group formed with the mission of introducing to the U.S. all of the birds mentioned in the works of Shakespeare. In the play *Henry IV*, a starling is mentioned and thus, in 1890, about 60 starlings were imported to the United States from Europe and subsequently released in New York City's Central Park. Another 40 starlings were released within a year and today the starling population in the United States is estimated at more than 200 million birds. Clearly, the starling is here to stay.

Breeding and Migration

Starlings (*Sturnus vulgaris*) are one of the most common birds in Europe and are most frequently described as robin-sized

Figure 6.1   The first European starling was introduced in New York's Central Park more than a hundred years ago. Since then, this invasive bird has expanded its range and has displaced native birds.

black birds with small white spots all over their bodies (Figure 6.1). The beak is brown in the winter and turns to yellow when the mating season approaches.

Female starlings are dominant perhaps because of the ratio of two females for every one male. Males attract females by song; male starlings with the more involved songs are considered more desirable to hens. Males will often imitate sounds they hear; male starlings will copy the songs of other birds and also mechanical sounds, and add these notes to their song repertoire.

The preferred winter roosting habitat is evergreen forest, specifically spruce, although these birds appear to be somewhat flexible. Starlings are mostly ground feeders and are often an important prey species for raptors (birds of prey) such as peregrine falcons and other hawks.

Economic Impact of Starlings

Starlings tend to be attracted to higher protein feeds and, to the dismay of farmers, may selectively consume them. In addition, the birds contaminate livestock water sources with their droppings.

Starlings can transfer a virus, TGE (transmissible gastroenteritis), to livestock. TGE passes through the digestive tract of starlings and the feces then become infectious. This virus can also be transmitted on boots or vehicles or by infected swine added to the herd. Starlings can also cause a respiratory disease in humans. A person can get this disease by breathing fungal spores from starling fecal matter. The fungus may grow in soils beneath bird roosts. Spores can become airborne in dry conditions.

Starlings cause other agricultural damage by eating cultivated fruits such as grapes and cherries. In some areas, they pull sprouting wheat and other grains from the soil to eat the planted seed.

Starling Management

To most people, all birds seem fairly harmless and for this reason, aggressive attempts to get rid of starlings or to their numbers are often met with public opposition.

The presence of any starlings in the United States represents a potential threat to our ecosystem since they are not native.

Cleaning up spilled grain is an easy method of controlling the starling population. Changing the way livestock is fed is also an important management practice to reduce starlings and thus potential disease. Feeding on the ground should be replaced with bird-proof livestock feeders; these feeders have flip-tops so that birds cannot freely eat the grain. Starlings are also attracted to water and draining unnecessary water pools will reduce starling numbers.

Devices to frighten starlings away are another tool to keep them from crops and other troublesome locations. These devices include recorded distress calls, gas-powered exploders, lights, and chemical agents. Using more than one scare technique and varying the location and intensity improves the effectiveness.

Toxicants are not recommended to control starlings because birds of all species will be killed. Trapping is another method but will only control limited numbers of birds in a localized area.

LD50: Determining Lethal Levels of Pesticides

Every pesticide has a lethal dose listed on the label. This lethal dose is referred to as LD50 and refers to the lethal dose where 50 percent of the test population died. The test population is usually a mammal such as a rat. This number is represented as milligrams (mg) per kilogram (kg) of body weight where mg is the amount of the chemical and kg is the body weight of the person that is exposed. The lower the LD50, the more toxic the substance because less of the chemical is required to kill half of the population.

LD50 is based on experiments done by scientists as part of the documentation required to get a pesticide approved for use by the U.S. Environmental Protection Agency (EPA). EPA reviews each pesticide to protect human health and the environment. The products are then labeled with a signal word (Danger, Warning, Caution) to indicate how toxic they are. Danger is the most toxic; Warning is the next toxic level; and Caution is the least toxic. Many familiar products are much more toxic, meaning they have a lower LD50, than most pesticides. Salt and caffeine have LD50 levels that make them more toxic than many pesticides.

7 Emerald Ash Borer

ANYTHING BUT A GEM

• •

The park ranger takes a deep breath as he hikes his favorite trail in Northeastern Indiana and stops for a moment to take a sip of water under a beautiful ash tree. The weather is perfect. When he started the hike, it was cool enough for a jacket but now he is perspiring. He notices a D-shaped hole in the bark of a mature ash tree. At closer inspection, there are exit holes. His stomach sinks, remembering back to his days in forest pest control in Michigan. Peeling back the bark, he recoils at the familiar creamy white larvae. The ash trees are in serious trouble. He looks around and wonders how many of the other nearby ashes are infested with the emerald ash borer. It all depends on how early he caught the infestation. Troubled, he logs the location in his GPS unit so that he knows exactly where he is. He then calls the EAB hotline to report his findings.

THE INSECT AND THE ASH

The emerald ash borer (*Agrilus planipennis*), or EAB, is an exotic, wood-boring beetle, originally from Asia (Figure 7.1). This tiny, metallic green insect was accidentally introduced, probably on solid woodpacking material in cargo ships or airplanes. EAB targets ash trees and currently has spread to Ohio, Michigan, and Indiana. More than six million ash trees are now dead or dying in southeastern Michigan.[13]

Figure 7.1 The emerald ash borer found its way to the United States as an accidental hitchhiker on wood cargo. Millions of ash trees have suffered or died from this invasive, wood-boring insect.

It takes an astute observer to notice that a tree is infected because the insects do not swarm around the outside of the tree like termites. Typically the upper third of a tree will die back first, followed by a large number of shoots or sprouts arising below the dead portions of the trunk. The adult insects are only present from mid-May until late July.

Prevention of Ash Borer Infestation

One way to prevent new infestations is to stop planting ash trees. The ash tree is a popular landscaping choice and is often selected for parks, roadsides, and yards. Until this pest is managed, it is recommended to plant an alternative in states where there are known infestations.

In Search of a Parasitoid

It is unlikely that the EAB will be eradicated in the United States. Currently, the only treatment is to identify infected trees and destroy them. Conventional insecticides are not currently recommended because they would kill all insects, not just the EAB. Therefore, a suitable biological control agent would be one way to help manage existing populations. Scientists from USDA-APHIS, U.S. Forest Service, and Michigan State University went back to the beetle's native region in China to search for natural predators that might be imported to the United States.

American scientists worked with staff from the Chinese Academy of Forestry to locate populations of EAB in Beijing and Tianjin City. EAB is at low density in China and is considered only a periodic pest of ash mostly because of host plant resistance and natural enemies. Simply put, ash trees in China have evolved with EAB, so they are better equipped to handle damage from the insect.

Since 2002, several parasitoids of EAB have been discovered in China.[14] A **parasitoid** is an insect whose parasitic larvae will eventually kill its host. One parasitoid (*Spathius* spp.) was found parasitizing EAB larvae by depositing 1 to 20 eggs of its own per EAB larva. In some stands of ash, up to 90 percent of the EAB larvae were parasitized. (Interestingly, in the process of surveying EAB for parasites, new species of insects were found. This demonstrates how large the insect world is and how much more there is to discover.)

Other new species of parasitoids of EAB have been discovered with varying mechanisms for parasitizing. A few of these species are being studied in a quarantine facility in the United States to make sure they would not become a pest if they were released for the control of EAB. One measure of a successful biological control agent is that it will only consume the intended host, whether it is a plant or animal. Having many broods in one season is another indicator of success as an introduced biological control agent. The qualities of two of the parasitoids found in China (*Spathius* and *Tetrastichus*) seem to make them a potentially successful biological control agent for EAB.

Microbial Insecticides

Microbial insecticides are made from microscopic living organisms capable of killing specific insects. Microscopic living organisms or microbes include viruses, bacteria, protozoa, and fungi. Unlike most insecticides, microbial insecticides are very effective at killing just the pest. Most insecticides kill the pest but end up killing other insect species. This is a problem because beneficial insects can be inadvertently killed while trying to kill the pest. The ability to target a specific insect species for control is one benefit of microbial insecticides over conventional insecticides.

Microbial insecticides are more acceptable to the public because they are non-toxic to humans, wildlife, birds, fish, and other organisms except for the insects they are trying to target. These compounds also are biodegradable, which means they will break down in the environment, becoming undetectable after a period of decomposition. Perhaps most significantly, microbial insecticides could be used with the release of biological control agents, specifically insects. Generally, an insecticide would kill any biological control insect, possibly undoing any progress with pest control. Since microbial insecticides target specific species, other insects would be unharmed.

It is important to remember that nearly all animals have the potential to succumb to disease as a result of a bacterial pathogen; the emerald ash borer is no exception. *Bacillus thuringiensis* (Bt) is a bacterial pathogen of insects that is the active ingredient of registered insecticides. Insects die by consuming Bt-saturated leaves.

Figure 7.2 Burning infected trees is one way of controlling the spread of emerald ash borer since the insect lives in the bark.

Scientists have found another pathogen to control EAB. *Beauveria bassiana* (GHA) is a fungus. Knowing that fungi are important natural enemies of EAB, scientists began to study this fungal pathogen to potentially control EAB. GHA kills the EAB adults. This insecticide would have to be applied every year to control EAB.

Using Quarantine to Avoid Infestation

The Indiana Department of Natural Resources recommends burning all firewood to avoid spreading the insect (Figure 7.2). As mentioned, EAB lives in the bark of ash trees. More specifically, firewood must not be brought into any Indiana park from counties that have EAB. This is just one type of quarantining. Quarantining is a cheap, sensible way to prevent new infestations of exotic species.

Formosan Subterranean Termite

BUILDING NESTS, RECRUITING SOLDIERS

8

• • • • • • • • • • • • • • • • • • • •

In Lafayette, Louisiana, a woman ties bright orange tape around her old oak tree in front of her house. The orange tape serves as a marker. Last May, she began seeing swarms of yellowish-brown, flying insects at dusk while she sat on her porch. A scientist employed by the county used a probe to collect some insects and then had them identified. The scientist told the woman that the telltale sign of the Formosan subterranean termite (*Coptotermes formosanus*) versus a native termite is the presences of hairy wings. It was, in fact, the dreaded Formosan. The good news was that the homeowner was able to take part in an eradication program and have her tree treated for only $25.

ORIGIN AND DISTRIBUTION OF THE FORMOSAN SUBTERRANEAN TERMITE

The Formosan subterranean termite (FST) is considered one of the most destructive termites in the world. FST was most likely accidentally imported into the United States through military installations after World War II. FST was then transported from ports to the interior cities by railroad ties and architectural timbers such as old beams, doors, and window frames. Railroad ties are structures that are used as a foundation for the rails of the track.

Native to China, this termite was introduced to Japan, Guam, Sri Lanka, South Africa, Hawaii, and the southern United States. Once introduced, swarming is the termite's main method of spread. However, this termite does not spread rapidly under its own power since it tends to be a weak flier. Rather, the transport of wood, trees, and landscaping materials is the primary method of long-range travel.

Formosan Subterranean Termite Damage

In most parts of the United States, termites are perhaps the single most damaging insect to homes. Termite inspections are customary prior to someone buying a home because of the high

Who's Who in the Termite World?

One of the first steps to control an invasive species is to find out how large the population is and its distribution. This is no small task when it comes to the Formosan subterranean termite (FST) since its identification from other termite species requires the skills of an entomologist.

In Louisiana, scientists were presented with the quandary of how they would go about determining an accurate distribution of the FST. At the time, there were many unconfirmed reports of FST in Louisiana. Scientists wanted a true account of FST distribution, so they did a survey and enlisted the support of other pest control agencies as well as the New Orleans Termite Control Board and the Louisiana Department of Agriculture.

In 1999, scientists sent out letters to pest management professionals and pest control districts throughout Louisiana asking if they would help collect termites for identification. If the respondent cost of replacing structural components that have been hollowed out by termites. An inspector bangs on the wood structure to determine if there is termite damage. In some cases, the full extent of termite damage is only revealed when the removal of drywall reveals the scurry of these insidious winged creatures. Given this, it is hard to believe that there is a termite even more aggressive than the termite native to the United States: the Formosan subterranean termite.

In Louisiana alone, this termite causes an estimated $500 million in damage (Figure 8.1). Now established in 11 states, including California and Hawaii, the pest costs an estimated $1 billion annually in property damage, repairs, and control.

indicated that they were willing to participate, they were sent a pack with individually numbered vials filled with alcohol, data sheets, return padded envelopes, and a handheld aspirator. The scientists had enough participants to get an approximate distribution of FST in Louisiana. Compared with previous surveys they were able to determine that FST infestations in Louisiana had significantly increased since 1966. They were also able to determine that many of these newer, confirmed infestations have remained relatively localized, and state officials have begun to target these areas for immediate treatment.*

*Matthew Messenger, Nan-Yao Su, and Rudolf H. Scheffran. "Current Distribution of the Formosan Subterranean Termite and Other Termite Species (Isoptera: Rhinotermitidae, Kalotermitidae) in Louisiana." *Florida Entomologist.* (December 2002): 580–587.

Figure 8.1 The Formosan subterranean termite is originally from China and is one of the most destructive termites in the world. This termite has been known to hollow out entire trees with its hearty appetite for cellulose.

These termites satisfy their appetite for cellulose by attacking the bases of poles, old tree stumps, or any other wood in contact with the soil, including homes. Most termites feed along the grain of the wood, selecting the softest parts of the wood first. The Formosan subterranean termites are less finicky eaters and have been known to hollow tree trunks or wooden beams.

Their diet also includes living plants such as citrus, pecan, and wild cherry trees. Oddly, Formosan subterranean termites supposedly will attack—but not eat—thin sheets of lead or copper, asphalt, plaster, mortar, rubber, and plastic in the search for food and moisture.

The termite nests are either in the ground or aerial and consist of chewed wood, saliva, and excrement. Formosan subterranean termites nests are often constructed where they have eaten the wood away and roughly resemble a carton because of their hollow interior. In Hawaii, there are accounts of homes that were built over colonies of termites that had major structural damage in six months and were completely destroyed in two years.

Their Royal Community

Termites are social creatures that live in societies with members having different functions, similar to fire ants (Figure 8.2). Like other social insects, they are characterized by cooperation in the rearing of the young, sharing of food, water, and shelter, an overlapping of generations, and a division of labor, characterized by the castes or life forms. A termite's colony consists of approximately equal numbers

Figure 8.2 Formosan subterranean termites live in a caste system of workers, soldiers, and reproductive individuals. Shown is a subterranean termite soldier.

of male and female young with just a few adults (king and queen).

A caste system exists in the termite community: physically distinct individuals perform different tasks in the highly structured termite society. The three castes are workers, soldiers, and reproductive individuals.

Workers are physically and sexually immature and most numerous in the community. Workers are wingless, white, blind, and typically the first termites seen when a piece of wood is infested. Winged termites are called "alates" and are yellowish-brown (Figure 8.3).

Formosan termites tend to hang out in clumps. If they were found in a tree, they would be more likely concentrated in trees in a small area rather than spread among trees throughout an entire neighborhood; this is why they are referred to as social insects.

FORMOSAN SUBTERRANEAN TERMITE CONTROL

Due to the high cost of FST damage, the United States Department of Agriculture, Agricultural Research Service (USDA/ARS) decided to launch Operation Full Stop, a $5 million-per-year national campaign to stop the termite by initiating cooperative agreements with other agencies, organizations, and universities. Scientists realize FST is here to stay in the United States and therefore have settled on an immediate goal of minimizing its destruction with population-management techniques and to wipe out individual colonies within a large geographical area. Other goals include improving detection, precision placement of termiticides, discovering and using biological control agents, and gaining new knowledge of this pest's biology and behavior.[15]

Figure 8.3 Formosan subterranean termites are social insects. The winged termites, or alates, are easy to spot near infestations. Alates are reproductive termites.

Termiticides and Baits

Termites are killed by injecting a termiticide into the trees where the insects are living. Termiticides are pesticides specifically designed to kill termites. This selectivity is significant since many insecticides kill all insects, which restricts their use.

Holes are bored in the tree and chemical foam is injected into rotten cavities. This technique alone provides a 60 to 70 percent control rate. To get a complete kill, a trench is dug around the tree and the chemicals are applied in the trench.

Scientists are looking at using FST's greedy appetite to entice it by using baits. This bait being studied to entice FST attracts them with essential nutrients that contain a poison to kill them. Some baits contain slow-acting toxins and others harbor insect growth-regulators that interfere with the way a termite forms and sheds its outer shell. The success of baits relies on the termites being willing to take the bait.

Natural Insecticides

Insecticides can be either synthetic or natural. Synthetic insecticides use compounds that were generated in a lab. Natural insecticides use compounds found in nature that are isolated for use. Most people feel more comfortable with chemicals that occur naturally. However, it is important to remember that many naturally occurring products, such as uranium, can also cause cancer.

Given the public's acceptance of natural insecticides, scientists have explored compounds that will kill FST. For example, vetiver is a fragrant grass used for erosion control and may kill FST with substances exuded from the plant's roots. Scientists have found many substances in the grass that repel or kill FST and are now looking at using the living grass as a barrier or repellent.

GENETIC SLEUTHING AND VIRTUAL MODELING

Operation Full Stop also funds research to better understand how this social insect lives. In some cases, people may think they have wiped out a colony of termites when remnants still are present nearby. When control is implemented in a specific geographic area, overlooking part of a colony can negate all efforts. To get a better sense of where a complete colony is, scientists use what they refer to as genetic sleuthing. Scientists are obtaining genetic "fingerprints" of FST in Louisiana, Florida, Texas, and Hawaii. It is impossible to differentiate termite populations by sight so DNA technology enables them to do what the naked eye cannot.[16] Although the same species would have very similar genetics, the different environments cause some genetic differences that can be discerned.

Genetic sleuthing will be able to determine how effective a treatment has been. With genetic testing, scientists can determine if the return of a termite population is the same one they thought they had killed or a completely different population that has moved in. Understanding the genetics of an insect can also help develop new insecticides.

Understanding the structure and design of the Formosan subterranean termite colony is another way to improve the effectiveness of treatments. Nan-Yao Su, an entomologist at the University of Florida, creates a virtual termite colony using computer-simulation models. Su is hoping that his models will predict the geometric patterns that characterize FST's tunneling in soils and then into homes.[17]

9 Winning the Battle Against Invasive Terrestrial Animals

It's called the Big Year, and it's all about how many different birds a person can see in a year. That's right: Big Year is an event in competitive birding. The competitors aren't all retired ladies either; one top competitor is an industrial contractor from New Jersey. In 1998, for the first time in history, three people saw 700 species of birds. Most die-hards spot 500 or so bird species. Sandy Komito was one of the lucky three. As imagined, competitive birding takes lots of dedication. Sandy spent more days traveling the continent to find birds than he spent at home. There were ptarmigans to trail in Colorado and hummingbirds to hunt in the hot Arizona desert. Even at night there was work to be done prowling for owls in the North Woods of Minnesota.[18] His endeavor required him to trade his typical day-to-day life for early mornings at chain restaurants, feverishly checking the Internet for rare-bird alerts. What Sandy is searching for is biological diversity. In a world without diversity, there would be just a handful of bird species to find. And no Big Year competition.

PRESERVING BIODIVERSITY

Biological diversity or **biodiversity** refers to the richness of life-forms in nature. The more diversified the life-forms are in an ecosystem, the more resilient it will be and therefore the more stable.

Invasive terrestrial animals threaten the biodiversity of our landscape. Instead of animals with specific, narrow functions and habitat requirements, international travel is introducing and accommodating the aggressive generalist. A generalist species is one that can live in a variety of habitats. This makes them a worthy adversary in a new environment.

Opinions vary on exactly how destructive invasive species are, but most naturalists embrace the lofty notion that all species have value and to lose them haphazardly by shuffling invaders around the globe is foolish. In some cases, we may be losing species that we have yet to discover, and that is like throwing away a good book before it has been read. One of the great challenges to the spread of invasive species is changing people's perceptions and increasing awareness about the issue.

PUBLIC INFORMATION CAMPAIGNS

Many people are not able to explain what an invasive species is. After a brief explanation, many people will say something like, "Oh, like the Africanized honey bee or love bug in Florida or the German cockroach." Radio, newspaper, and television have increased knowledge about this important environmental topic but work still needs to be done to increase awareness. An informed public is crucial to controlling invasive terrestrial animals. Public information campaigns raise awareness about a particular issue through the use of media. A message to conserve water or electricity is one example of a public information campaign with an environmental emphasis.

Challenges to Environmental Campaigns

Environmental campaigns have three main obstacles: 1) a lack of resources to conduct sophisticated advertising campaigns; 2) constraints on acceptable types of appeals that might limit use of fear, humor, or anything other than direct presentation of information; and 3) the need to communicate large amounts of information that prevents subtle forms of communication.[19] There is less of a sense of immediate accomplishment from changing behavior as a result of an environmental campaign. Another obstacle is the attempt to communicate relatively complex scientific principles to the general public. For example, people seem to want quick and easy answers to questions such as "Why are invasive species bad?" A scientist would answer "Invasive species lack natural predators and therefore disrupt ecosystem processes." This answer stands little chance of being

Invasive Species and Our National Parks

According to the National Parks and Conservation Association (NPCA), invasive species are present in nearly 200 of our national parks and wildlife refuges. In the Everglades, native fish populations are declining because of the Asian swamp eel (*Monopterus albus*). In Yellowstone National Park, exotic lake trout are killing off native cutthroat trout species. Grizzly bears are finding their food source dwindling as a result, since the exotic trout swim at much deeper depths than the native trout.

Many federal agencies recognize the problem of invasive species, but action requires public comment, which lengthens the time before something can be done. The best approach generally involves multiple agencies working together.

When the Asian swamp eel was discovered by some children at a nature center within a mile of the Everglades National Park, natural resource professionals knew they had to act quickly. The United States Geological Survey (USGS), U.S. Fish and Wildlife Service (USFWS), understood by the general public. The challenge is to find a way to communicate in a manner that a nonscientist can interpret. But the challenge does not end here. Conservation messages strive to not only convey the information but to encourage a response.

People have a natural predisposition to expose themselves to messages that are in agreement with their currently held beliefs and attitudes. A currently held belief about an environmental message such as the threat of invasive species might be that invasive species are just part of the natural cycle and that we shouldn't try to manipulate nature.

and Florida Game and Freshwater Fish Commission got together to form a work group to minimize the eel's impact on the Everglades. The Asian swamp eel thrives in shallow wetlands, marshes, streams, ditches, and ponds. This exotic species can breathe under water like a fish but can also slither across dry land, sucking air through a two-holed snout. The swamp eel is a predator that feeds on small aquatic organisms yet can survive weeks, possibly months without food. The swamp eel also appears virtually unaffected by explosives and poisons used for eradication.

Due to the resilience of this invasive species, the group knew they needed a comprehensive strategy to control the eel. One part of the strategy was to determine the current distribution; another focused on ways to prevent further spread, and yet another allocated resources for research into the most effective methods of control. When an invasive species newly invades any ecosystem, rapid response increases the likelihood of eradication or at least containment.

Personal and Collective Benefits of Changing Behavior

If people perceive that their health is threatened by an environmental problem, then they are more likely to change their behavior as a result of an information campaign. Some environmental issues, such as toxic waste, are perceived as a threat, particularly by women who have young children. However, the perception of a *personal* threat is unlikely for many environmental problems. This is yet another disadvantage to environmental public information campaigns. Many important social problems involve collective benefits such as a campaign to stop littering, yet most campaigns have succeeded only when they promote individual benefits.

Message Appeal

The type of appeal in an environmental message has different effects depending on the message. Scientists coined the terms "sick baby" versus "well baby" appeals.[20] The "baby is sick" appeal focuses on the problem and emphasizes the problem's severity. The "baby is well" appeal is an affirmation of the individual's action and the potential for significant effect. The latter approach works by increasing the belief that one can do something to solve the problem. An example of these two appeals follows:

Sick Baby Appeal

Seattle is facing a water shortage. This summer's water crisis could be the worst in the history of the region. Normally, at this time of year, there are 80 inches of snowpack in the mountains. That snow would melt gradually during the summer, replenishing the reservoirs. The lack of snowfall, a warm winter, and spring weather have created an ominous threat. Unless everyone stops watering lawns, installs low-flow showerheads, and takes care to reduce water waste, we face a drought this summer. The public service advertising agency asks you PLEASE CONSERVE WATER.

Well Baby Appeal

Seattle is facing a water shortage. The lack of snowfall, a warm winter, and spring weather have reduced water reserves. But, the city will have sufficient water for the summer if each person takes individual responsibility for reducing water waste. With very little change in daily routine or lifestyle, each person could reduce water use by 10 gallons per day. If everyone stops watering lawns, installs low-flow showerheads, and takes care to reduce water waste, we can avoid a drought this summer. The public service advertising agency asks you PLEASE CONSERVE WATER.

These two examples clearly show the differences in the messages regarding the environmental issue of water conservation. Subjects were read either the well baby or sick baby message and than asked a series of questions such as "How likely is it that the communication above would influence you to take steps to conserve water?"

The well baby appeal was more effective in motivating people to conserve water. The well baby appeal affirms the individual's action and its potential for significant effect. This appeal works by increasing the belief that one can do something to solve the problem. The sick baby appeal works by increasing concern and perhaps may make the problem seem overwhelming and insolvable to many people. The success of the well baby appeal operates through its affirmation of the significance of individual action. However, with issues that are less well known, such as the over-accumulation of solid waste, the sick baby appeal offers advantages by increasing the level of concern.

Communication Channels to Reach People

It is important to determine your audience before deciding how to communicate a message. High school students rated television as a more prevalent source of environmental information than magazines or newspapers. Broadcast news, such as a Jacques Cousteau special, increases knowledge for two weeks after the program but awareness returns to the pre-viewing levels after two weeks. Repetition seems necessary to cause a more lasting behavior change. Despite this, television and film seem to be able to alter attitudes. This potential influence, combined with an effective transmission of knowledge, could prove beneficial to a campaign about invasive species.

Another way an invasive species information campaign could be communicated is through a theme or package. Themes or packages can help provide definition to an amorphous topic but represent more significant commitment of station resources. Information supplied for free such as news releases, reports, and tips can greatly decrease the resources expended by news teams and amount to an "information subsidy." In addition, reporters may have little expertise in an area such as the danger of invasive species and therefore they need more information from outside sources.

Smokey Bear's Success

The Smokey Bear campaign was created in 1944 by the Ad Council at the request of the U.S. Forest Service (Figure 9.1). This campaign was a huge success and, according to the Ad Council, reduced the number of acres lost annually to forest fires by 82 percent. This campaign succeeded in at least familiarizing people with the issue of forest fire prevention.

As mentioned, campaigns are likely to succeed when they portray a central theme of the individual's efforts being needed. The Smokey Bear ad campaign did that through the slogans

Figure 9.1 Public information campaigns are an excellent way to raise awareness about an environmental problem. The Smokey Bear campaign was a huge success and reduced forest fires by 82 percent.

"Only You Can Prevent Forest Fires" and "Smokey is Counting On You," as captions under the picture of Smokey Bear with a shovel in hand or his finger pointing. It also appeals to the idea of a perceived threat, another criterion for a successful campaign, perhaps not so much to people as to wildlife. One ad used a stamp displaying a frightened bear cub up a burnt tree clinging for dear life with the shadow of Smokey in the background. It is relatively easy to motivate individuals to action when adorable, furry animals are depicted to be in peril due to human actions.

Another reason why this campaign succeeded was because the audience was aware of forest fires and ready to accept the message. This level of audience awareness makes it unnecessary to break commonly held beliefs.

However, there have been some problems with this campaign such as educating the public on the value of fire in a forest ecosystem. Ironically, the Forest Service has in recent years faced some public opposition to prescribed burns, perhaps because of the success of the Smokey Bear campaign.

A SUCCESSFUL INVASIVE SPECIES CAMPAIGN

As the Smokey Bear example shows, understanding your audience is crucial to developing an effective message. However, despite all of the research, audiences remain an enigma. Research is needed to estimate how much the average person knows about invasive species. Surveys are one way to find out what people think or know about them.

Developing an effective message and motivational techniques for a successful campaign is a complex interaction among the environmental issue, the prominence of the issue, and the audience. If an issue is familiar, then a "well baby" appeal is more effective in causing behavior change. If not, then the "sick baby" appeal will generate favorable attitudes toward action. One type of action that an invasive species campaign might address is for people to report the sighting of an invasive animal or plant. Knowing early on when an invasive species has been sighted saves a tremendous amount of resources in control efforts.

The northern snakehead (*Channa argus*) is a fish native to Asia that can breathe air and wriggle across land. It is a predatory species that has a voracious appetite for fish and frogs. A fisherman discovered an early introduction of the northern snakehead in waters bordering New Jersey and Pennsylvania. Out one day fishing, an angler caught a fish that was unfamiliar to him. He took a picture of it, put it on the Internet, and posed the question to other sportsmen asking what it was. His early identification of a highly invasive fish enabled natural resource professionals to act before the fish caused serious problems. Going one step further, an effective information campaign would educate people first about what to look out for instead of relying on them to be curious and find out what a species is.

Unfortunately, simply making people aware of an environmental problem may not result in action. An invasive species campaign would be more effective if there is a perception of personal environmental threat. Techniques such as social pressure result in only temporary behavior changes. A lasting behavior change requires an emphasis on the individual. In the case of the curious angler who discovered the snakehead, it really did take only one person to make a difference in the battle against invasive species.

CONCLUSION

Invasive terrestrial animals are like bullies in nature's playground. They don't play by the rules—they lack natural predators to keep them in check. Guam's brown treesnake has decimated that island's birds. The wild boar has destroyed precious wetlands in the southeastern United States by eating all vegetation in its path. The wild boar also alters the ecosystem by creating wallows to stay cool, which leads to soil erosion.

Ecological implications aside, these animals degrade our enjoyment of the outdoors. Patrons at the Tree Bar in Guam could no longer enjoy themselves because of all of the brown treesnakes that dangled from the tree that the bar was named for and the staff was forced to cut it down. Periodic power outages caused by the snakes are annoying and not good for a country that relies on

Careers in Wildlife

Wildlife is a valuable resource that often requires protection. The conservation of wildlife on public lands is the responsibility of federal, state, and local governments. People who choose to work in wildlife management need to have skills in working with people, not just wildlife. In many cases, professionals must work to find a solution to wildlife damage before people attempt a solution on their own that may be ecologically damaging. In New Jersey, roaming black bears are a common complaint by residents. An educational campaign was initiated by the New Jersey Department of Environmental Protection to provide information about ways to reduce conflicts between bears and people including brochures with information on such things as tips on bear-proofing your trash.

Jobs at agencies such as the Animal and Plant Health Inspection Service (APHIS), include wildlife specialists, wildlife biologists, and wildlife research biologists. Wildlife specialists work to ensure that control methods are being used correctly and to record success or failure of that method. Job duties include tourism as a revenue generator. Imported fire ants have ruined many a picnic just as the Formosan subterranean termite hollows out wooden structures and kills neighborhood trees.

The solution involves prevention, research, education, regulation, and implementing management tools. Preventative strategies such as quarantining and inspections at ports and other entry points are well-directed efforts for invasive terrestrial animals. Killing animals, whether invasive or native, is not something that everyone feels comfortable with. Preventing invasions eliminates the necessity to make that choice. In

trapping and relocating birds and mammals that cause damage to agriculture or natural resources.

Wildlife biologists develop wildlife management plans. In Nebraska, wildlife biologists helped protect two endangered birds, the Interior least tern and the Three-lined piping plover, while biologists in Ohio, Texas, and Vermont helped stop the spread of rabies.

Wildlife research biologists conduct experiments on issues such as contraception delivered by vaccination and the use of repellents, electronic trap-monitoring devices, and habitat modification to control wildlife damage.

The best way to get a sense of what a career would be like is to volunteer. Another option is to request an informational interview to assess what a position's day-to-day responsibilities are. Internships also provide great experience, professional contacts, and in some cases, college credit. If interested in positions with APHIS, visit http://www.aphis.usda.gov.

addition, wildlife control staff will not have to explain unpopular decisions such as the mass killing of starlings to the public.

Research can help devise better ways to control these invasive animals. Baits and termiticides offer control of invasive animals with the use of chemicals. Parasitoids are one example of biological control where the pest's natural enemy is introduced —with caution—to attempt to control the invasive animal. Foolhardy introductions such as the cane toad no longer occur because the USDA/APHIS is extremely careful about introducing an exotic species to control another exotic species. In Australia, rabbits are a significant problem and scientists have introduced a virus that was specific to these invaders. This virus was specifically engineered to be highly infectious to rabbits only. This is another form of biological control that only research can develop.

Educating the public will help to elicit public support and participation. Maryland and Virginia state officials partnered with sporting goods stores to organize a northern snakehead derby, offering rewards to anglers catching this invasive fish.

USDA/APHIS is the federal agency with the responsibility for preventing invasive terrestrial animals from entering this country through ports as well as other entry points. The APHIS inspection process to prevent invasives from entering this country is well-focused energy.

Currently, the United States is holding its own when it comes to the spread of invasive terrestrial animals. It is a daily struggle to keep invasive species out of the country. Research, funding, and outreach must be increased in order to do better than simply maintaining the status quo.

NOTES

1. Barbara Terkanian, *A Natural History of the Sonoran Desert*, Arizona Sonora Desert Museum, 2002, p. 1.

2. Neil A. Campbell and Jane B. Reece, *The Tree of Life: An Introduction to Biological Diversity.* Seventh Edition. Berkeley, CA: Pearson Education, 2005, p. 529.

3. Gilbert Waldbauer, *What Good Are Bugs?* Cambridge, Mass.: Harvard University Press, 2003, p. 1.

4. Steve Jones, *Darwin's Ghost.* New York: Random House, 1999, p. 149.

5. James K. Wangberg, *Six-Legged Sex: The Erotic Lives of Bugs.* Golden, Colo.: Fulcrum Publishing, 2001, p. 24.

6 Steve Jones, *Darwin's Ghost.* New York: Random House, 1999, p. 46.

7. Adrian Forsyth and Ken Miyata, *Tropical Nature.* New York: Charles Scribner's Sons, 1984, pp. 153-167.

8. Andy Holdsworth, Cindy Hale, and Lee Frelich, *Earthworms.* University of Minnesota Center for Hardwood Ecology. Minnesota Department of Natural Resources. March 2003. Available online at: http://www.dnr.state.mn.us/invasives/terrestrial animals/earthworms.

9. L. Greenberg, J. Klotz, and J. Kabashima, *Red Imported Fire Ant.* Davis, Cal.: IPM Education and Publications, 2001, p.2.

10. Timothy Lockley, *Imported Fire Ants.* Imported Fire Ant Station, USDA/APHIS/PPQ. Gulfport: Miss. Available online at: http://www.ipmworld.umn.edu/chapters/lockley.htm.

11. Thomas H. Fritts and D. Leasman-Tanner, *The Brown Treesnake on Guam: How the Arrival of One Invasive Species Damaged the Ecology, Commerce, Electrical Systems, and Human Health on Guam: A Comprehensive Information Source.* 200l. Available online at http://www.fort.usgs.gov/resources/education/bts/bts_home.asp.

12. Thomas H. Fritts, "Freshwater Foundation." *Aquatic Nuisance Species Digest* 24, no.1 (November 2000). Navarre, Minn. Available online at: http://www.anstaskforce.gov/ANSDigest-Feb01.pdf.

13. David Smitley and Deborah McCullough, *How Homeowners Can Protect Ash Trees from the Emerald Ash Borer in Southeastern Michigan.* Michigan State University. 2004. Available online at: http://www.emeraldashborer.info/files/Howtoprotectashtrees3-04.pdf.

14. Juli Gould, Leah Bauer, Houping Liu, Dave Williams, Paul Schaefer, and Dick Reardon, *Potential for Biological Control of the Emerald Ash Borer.* USDA Forest Service. Available online at: http://www.emeraldashborer.info.

15. USDA/ARS, "Taking Aim at Formosan Subterranean Termites." *Agricultural Research.* October 2000. Available online at: http://www.ars.usda.gov.

16. Ibid.

17. Ibid.

18. Mark Obmascik, *The Big Year.* New York: Free Press, 2004, p. 1.

19. C. Obermiller, "The Baby is Sick/the Baby is Well: A Test of Environmental Communication Appeals." *Journal of Advertising* 24, 1995: pp. 55–68.

20. Ibid., p. 60.

GLOSSARY

Animalia One of the five kingdoms. It includes organisms with a hollow body cavity such as a jellyfish; worms with segmented bodies; arthropods, which have exoskeletons and jointed legs, such as grasshoppers, lobsters, and spiders; and vertebrates such as humans and other mammals, birds, reptiles, amphibians, and fish.

Annelids Worms with segmented bodies.

Arthropods Animals that have exoskeletons and jointed legs, such as grasshoppers, lobsters, and spiders.

Ballast water The material that ships take up to maintain stability during transport.

Biological control The method of introducing an invasive species' natural predator.

Biological diversity or biodiversity The richness of life-forms in nature.

Botany The study of plants.

Carnivores Animals that kill and eat other animals; they eat both herbivores and omnivores.

Coelenterates Organisms with a hollow body cavity such as a jellyfish.

Chordates Organisms with a nerve chord and usually a backbone, such as humans and other mammals, birds, reptiles, amphibians, and fish.

Commensalism A relationship between two species where one species benefits and the other is unaffected.

Entomology The study of insects.

Feral   A previously domesticated animal that is living in the wild.

Fungi   One of the five kingdoms. It includes mushrooms, molds, and mildews.

Herbivores   Animals that get their energy from consuming only plants.

Heterotrophs   Animals that cannot derive energy from sunlight or inorganic chemicals; they feed on other life-forms.

Host-specific   Refers to biological control insects that will only attack one plant or host.

Invertebrates   Animals without backbones.

Molting   The process of shedding an exterior coating to reveal new growth.

Monera   One of the five kingdoms. It includes bacteria and blue-green algae.

Mutually beneficial or mutualism   A relationship between two organisms where both benefit.

Obligate brood parasite   A bird species that has completely abandoned the task of building nests, incubating eggs, and feeding and rearing nestlings. These birds invade the nests of other birds to lay their eggs and the host rears the nestlings.

Omnivores   Organisms that eat both meat and plants; some will hunt for their food while others scavenge for dead animals.

Parasitism   A relationship between two organisms where one organism benefits, the parasite, to the detriment of the host; the parasite generally does not kill its host.

Parasitoid   An insect whose parasitic larvae will eventually kill its host.

Plantae   One of the five kingdoms. It includes mosses, ferns, and flowering plants.

Plant pathology   The study of plant disease.

Protista   One of the five kingdoms. It includes mostly unicellular organisms including algae and amoebas.

Vertebrates   Animals with backbones.

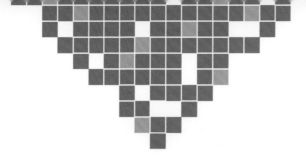

BIBLIOGRAPHY

Backes, D. "The biosocial perspective and environmental communication research." *Journal of Communication* 45 (1995): 147–163.

Baldassare, M. and Katz, C. "The personal threat of environmental problems as predictor of environmental practices." *Environment and Behavior* 24, no. 5 (1992): 606–615.

Berenbaum, May R. *Ninety-nine Gnats, Nits, and Nibblers.* Chicago, Il: University of Illinois Press, 1990.

Campbell, Neil A. and Jane B. Reece. *The Tree of Life: An Introduction to Biological Diversity.* 7th ed. Berkeley, CA: Pearson Education, 2005.

Corbett, J. B. "The environment as theme and package on a local television newscast." *Science Communication* 19, no. 3 (1998): 222–237.

DeYoung, R. "Changing behavior and making it stick: The conceptualization and management of conservation behavior." *Environment and Behavior* 25, no. 4 (1993): 485–505.

Forest Fire Prevention. Ad Council. 1999. Available online. http://www.adcouncil.org/body_camp_historic_fire.html.

Forsyth, Adrian and Ken Miyata. *Tropical Nature.* New York: Charles Scribner's Sons, 1984.

Fritts, Thomas H. "Problems and innovations in controlling Brown Treesnakes on Guam." *Aquatic Nuisance Species Digest* 4, no. 1 (November 2000): 1–4.

Fritts, T. H. and D. Leasman-Tanner. *The Brown Treesnake on Guam.* 2001. Available online at: http://www.fort.usgs.gov/resources/education/bts/bts_home.asp.

Gaudette, Karen. "Marching by the millions." *The Daily University of Washington.* January 20, 1999. Available online at: http://www.archives.thedaily.washington.edu/1999.

Gould, Juli, Leah Bauer, Houping Liu, Dave Williams, Paul Schaefer, and Dick Reardon. *Potential for Biological Control of the Emerald Ash Borer.* USDA Forest Service. Available online at:http://www.emeraldashborer.info.

Greenberg, L., J. Klotz, and J. Kabashima. *Red Imported Fire Ant.* Davis, Cal.: IPM Education and Publications, 2001.

Hamilton, L. C. "Concern about toxic wastes: three demographic predictors." *Sociological Perspectives* 28, no. 4 (1995): 463–486.

Heath, R. L., Seshadri, S., and Lee, Jaesub. "Risk communication: A two-community analysis of proximity, dread, trust, involvement, uncertainty, openness/accessibility, and knowledge on support/opposition toward chemical companies." *Journal of Public Relations Research* 10, no. 1 (1998): 35–56.

Holdsworth, Andy, Cindy Hale, and Lee Frelich. "Earthworms." University of Minnesota Center for Hardwood Ecology. Minnesota Department of Natural Resources. March 2003. Available online at: http:// www.dnr.state.mn.us/invasives/terrestrialanimals/earthworms.

Jones, Steve. *Darwin's Ghost.* New York: Random House, 1999.

Kemple, Megan. "ABCs of toxicology." *Journal of Pesticide Reform* 21, no. 4 (Winter 2001).

Lockley, Timothy. *Imported Fire Ants.* Imported Fire Ant Station, USDA/APHIS/PPQ. Gulfport: MS. Available online at: http://www.ipmworld.umn.edu/chapters/lockley.htm.

Messenger, Matthew, Nan-Yao Su, and Rudolf H. Scheffrahn. "Current distribution of the formosan subterranean termite and other termite species (*Isoptera: Rhinotermitidae, Kalotermitidae*) in Louisiana." *Florida Entomologist.* 2002.

National Biological Information Infrastructure and Invasive Species Specialist Group. "Ecology of *Molothrus bonariensis.*" 2005. Available online at: http:// www.invasivespecies.net.

Obermiller, C. "The baby is sick/the baby is well: A test of environmental communication appeals." *Journal of Advertising* 24, no. 2 (1995): 55–68.

Obmascik, Mark. *The Big Year.* New York: Free Press, 2004.

Rice, R. E. and Atkin, C. "Principles of Successful Public Communication Campaigns." In *Media Effects: Advances in Theory and Research.* J. Bryant and D. Zillman (eds.) Mahwah, NJ: Lawrence Erlbaum Associates, Publishers, 1994: 365–387.

Rogers, C. L. "The Importance of Understanding Audiences." In S. M. Friedman, S. Dunwoody, and C. L. Rogers (eds.), *Communicating Uncertainty.* Mahwah, NJ: Lawrence Erlbaum Associates, Publishers, 1999: 179–200.

Rowan, K. E. "Effective Explanation of Uncertain and Complex Science." In S.M. Friedman, S. Dunwoody, & C. L. Rogers (eds.), *Communicating Uncertainty.* Mahwah, NJ: Lawrence Erlbaum Associates, Publishers, 1999: 201–223.

Severin, W. J. and Tankard, J. W. *Communication Theories: Origins, Methods, and Uses in the Mass Media.* 5th ed. White Plains, NY: Longman, 2001: 80–82.

Smitley, David and Deborah McCullough. *How Homeowners Can Protect Ash Trees From the Emerald Ash Borer in Southeastern Michigan.* Michigan State University, 2004.

Terkanian, B. *A Natural History of the Sonoran Desert.* Arizona Sonora Desert Museum, 2002.

USDA/APHIS Wildlife Services. *Recovering Threatened and Endangered Species, Guarding Against Invasive Species, Preserving Wildlife and Game Habitats.* Available online at: http://www.usda.aphis.gov.

USDA/ARS. "Taking aim at formosan subterranean termites." *Agricultural Research.* October 2000. Available online at: http://www.ars.usda.gov.

Waldbauer, Gilbert. *Millions of Monarchs, Bunches of Beetles.* Cambridge, Mass.: Harvard University Press, 2000.

Waldbauer, G. *What Good Are Bugs?* Cambridge, Mass.: Harvard University Press, 2003.

Zimmerman, L.K. "Knowledge, affect, and the environment: 15 years of research (1979–1993)." *Journal of Environmental Education* 27, no. 3 (1996): 41–44.

FURTHER READING

Baskin, Y. *A Plague of Rats and Rubbervines: The Growing Threat of Species Invasions.* Covelo, Cal.: Shearwater Books, 2003.

Berenbaum, May R. *Ninety-nine Gnats, Nits, and Nibblers.* Chicago, Il: University of Illinois Press, 1990.

Cox, G. *Alien Species and Evolution: The Evolutionary Ecology of Exotic Plants, Animals, Microbes and Interacting Native Species.* Washington, D.C.: Island Press, 2004.

Forsyth, A. and K. Miyata. *Tropical Nature.* New York: Charles Scribner's Sons, 1984.

Mooney, H. A. *Invasive Species in a Changing World.* Washington, D.C.: Island Press, 2000.

Waldbauer, Gilbert. *Millions of Monarchs, Bunches of Beetles.* Cambridge, Mass.: Harvard University Press, 2000.

Wilson, E. O. *The Diversity of Life.* Cambridge, Mass.: The Belknap Press of Harvard University, 1992.

_____. *The Future of Life.* New York: Vintage Publishing, 2003.

WEB SITES
Cornell University–Biological Control
http://www.nysaes.cornell.edu/ent/biocontrol/info/biocont.html

The Global Invasive Species Database
http://www.issg.org/database/welcome

The Nature Conservancy (TNC)–Invasive Species
http://www.nature.org/initiatives/invasivespecies

USDA Animal and Plant Health Inspection Service (APHIS)
http://www.aphis.usda.gov/ppq

USDA APHIS Pest Tracker
http://ceris.purdue.edu/napis/index.html

USDA National Invasive Species Information Center
http://www.invasivespeciesinfo.gov

The Wildlife Society
http://www.wildlife.org/policy/index.cfm?tname=positionstatements
&statement=ps14

Wisconsin Council on Invasive Species
http://invasivespecies.wi.gov/awareness

PICTURE CREDITS

page:

9: Dr. John D. Cunningham/Visuals Unlimited

10: Mary Clay/Dembinsky Photo Associates

13: USDA/ARS

17: Andy Williams/CritterZone

22: Peter Ambruzs/CritterZone

32: U.S. Geological Survey Archives, U.S.Geological Survey

38: Phil Degginer/Dembinsky Photo Associates

41: Scott Bauer/USDA/ARS

44: Daniel Wojcik/USDA/ARS

51: Robert Myers/Visuals Unlimited

52: Associated Press, AP

57: Leonard Lee Rue III/Visuals Unlimited

65: Lee Karney, U.S. Fish & Wildlife Service

69: David Cappaert, www.forestryimages.org

72: USDA Forest Service Archives, USDA Forest Service

76: USDA/ARS

77: Scott Bauer/USDA/ARS

79: Scott Bauer/USDA/ARS

89: Lisboa T/C

Cover: John Mitchell / Photo Researchers, Inc.

INDEX

A

acetaminophen, 54–55
agriculture, starlings and, 66
amphibians, overview of, 18–19
Anderson, John, 17
Animalia, 8, 10–11
annelids, defined, 8
antelope, 18
ants, 12, 14–15, 37–47
APHIS, 27–28, 49, 92–93, 94
arctic foxes, 8
Argentine ants, 42
arthropods, defined, 8
ash borers, 68–72
Asian swamp eels, 84–85
Australia, rabbits in, 35–36, 94
awareness, 83

B

Bacillus thuringiensis (Bt), 71
baiting, 45–46, 80, 94
ballast water, 38–39, 68
Beauveria bassiana (GHA), 72
beetles, 68–72
behavioral changes, 86–87
Berenbaum, May, 11
Big Year, birding and, 82
biodiversity, preservation of, 82–83
biological control, 31–34, 46–47, 70–72, 94
birds, 20–21, 52, 82
black imported fire ants. *See* fire ants
blackflies, parasitism and, 23–24
blindness, river, 23–24
boars
    biology and behavior of, 57–60
    domestication and, 36
    GPS technology and, 60–63
    management options for, 60–63

overview of problem, 56–57
reestablishment of in Britain, 61
borers, 68–72
botany, defined, 28
botflies, 22–23
Britain, wild boars and, 61
brood parasitism, 20–21
brown treesnakes
    control of, 27, 53–55
    economy and, 51–53
    humans and, 53
    native wildlife and, 50–51
    overview of, 48–50
brown-headed cowbird, 21
butterflies, commensalism and, 24

C

cane toads, lesson of, 31–34
careers in wildlife, 92–93
cargo ships, 38–39, 68
carnivores, defined, 20
caste system, termites and, 77–78
castings, defined, 17
caterpillars, 34–35
cellulose, 14, 76
challenges to environmental
    campaigns, 83–85
chemicals, 16, 32, 35, 67
Chinese Academy of Forestry, 70
chordates, defined, 8
coelenterates, defined, 8
commensalism, defined, 24
communication channels, 88–91
composting, 17–18
control methods
    for boars, 60–63
    for brown treesnakes, 53–55
    careers in, 92–93
    for emerald ash borers, 69–72

for fire ants, 44–47
for Formosan termites, 78–80
organizations for, 49
rapid response and, 85
for starlings, 66–67
corn earworm caterpillars, 34–35
cowbirds, brood parasitism and, 21
crocodiles, plovers and, 25
crops, damage to by fire ants, 40
cuckoo birds, 21

D
diversity, preservation of, 82–83
DNA fingerprinting, 80–81
domains, defined, 9–10
domesticated, feral vs., 34–36
dosages, LD50, 67
dry-wood termites, 13–14

E
earthworms, 16–18, 29–30
economy, 51–53, 66, 75, 78
ecosystems, fire ants and, 40–42
eels, in Everglades, 84–85
Egyptian plovers, 25
electrical currents, fire ants and, 43
emerald ash borers, 68–72
enemies, lack of, 29–30
entomology, defined, 11, 28
environmental campaigns, 83–85
EPA, LD50 determination and, 67
European starlings, 64–67
Everglades National Park, 84–85
evolution, 30–31
exoskeletons, 10–11
exploders, 67

F
feral animals, 34–36
fingerprinting, genetic, 80–81
fire, insects and, 31
fire ants
arrival of, 37–39
control of, 44–47
ecological influences of, 40–42
humans and, 42–43
life cycle of, 39–40
native, 43–44

fireflies, 15, 16
food chain, 12, 19–20
Forest Service, U.S., 27
Formosan subterranean termites
community structure of, 77–78
control methods for, 78–80
damage from, 74–77
genetics, modeling and, 80–81
origin and distribution of, 73–74
foxes, arctic, 8
fumigants, 54–55
fungi, 8, 72

G
gas-powered exploders, 67
genetic sleuthing, termites and, 80–81
GPS technology, boars and, 60–63
grasses, termite control and, 80
Great Smoky Mountains National
Park, 60–62
grizzly bears, trout and, 84
Guam. *See* brown treesnakes

H
Hawaii, 53, 55, 58–59
health, appeals to, 86–87
herbivores, defined, 19–20
heterotrophs, defined, 9
hogs, 36
honeypot ants, 14–15
host-specific predators, defined, 33
humans
brown treesnakes and, 53
fire ants and, 42–43
hunting and, 56–57, 60–62
influence of, 26–28
parasitism and, 21–24
hunting, 56–57, 60–62

I
iguanas, 18–19
imported fire ants. *See* fire ants
Indiana Department of Natural
Resources, 72
infochemicals, 15–16, 34–35
information gathering, 27–28
insecticides, 45, 71–72, 79–80
insects, 11–15, 15–16, 31

invasiveness
    domestication and, 31–34
    humans and, 26–28
    lack of enemies and, 29–30
    lessons of cane toad and, 31–34
    predator-prey relationships and,
        30–31
invertebrates, defined, 10
islands, 51, 58–59

K
kingdom classification, 8–10
kingfishers, 52
Komito, Sandy, 82

L
landscaping plants, 37
LD50, pesticides and, 67
life, kingdoms of, 8–10
Louisiana, termites in, 73, 74–75
luciferin and luciferase, 16

M
maggots, 22–23
Mammal Society, 61
mammals, overview of, 18
management options. *See* control
    methods
matriarchies, ants and, 42–43
memory, animals and, 19
message appeals, 86
Michigan, 68
microbial insecticides, 71–72, 80
Microdon, classification of, 12
Micronesian kingfishers, 52
milkweed, 24
Minnesota, worms in, 29–30
modeling, termites and, 80–81
mollusks, 10
monarch butterflies, 24
Monera, 8
mounds, fire ants and, 40–42
movement, 7, 26–27, 50
mutualism, 14, 25, 34–35

N
NASA, 27
National Parks, 84–85

Nature Conservancy, 49
northern snakeheads, 91

O
obstacles to environmental campaigns,
    83–85
omnivores, defined, 19–20
Operation Full Stop, 78, 80–81
oxen, 18

P
parasitism, 20–21, 21–24, 46
parasitoids, 69–71, 94
pathogens, 30
Peace Valley Nature Center, 64
perceived threats, 90
pesticides, LD50 and, 67
Pete's Bizarre Bazaar, 33
pharmacology, 33
pheromones, 15–16, 35
phorid flies, fire ant control and, 46
Photinus and *Photorus*, 15
phytosanitary certificates, 28
pigs. *See* boars
plant pathology, defined, 28
Plantae, 8
plants, damage to by fire ants, 40
plovers, mutualism and, 25
pollination, insects and, 12
potatoes, damage to by fire ants, 40
power outages, 51–52
predator-prey relationships, 30–31,
    50–51
Protista, 8
protozoans, 46–47
public information campaigns, 83–86,
    88–91

Q
quarantine, 72
queens, fire ant control and, 45

R
rabbits, in Australia, 35–36, 94
railroad ties, termites and, 73
razorbacks. *See* boars
recycling, insects and, 12–13
red fire ants. *See* fire ants

regulations, function of, 27–28
reproduction, of insects, 15–16
reptiles, overview of, 19
river blindness, 23–24
Rooshian hogs. *See* boars

S

saolas, 18
satellite imagery, 27, 62–63
Shakespeare, starlings and, 64
shiny cowbirds, 21
shipping, 38–39, 68
shrews, wild boars and, 60
sick baby appeals, 86–87
skeletons, terrestrial animals and, 7
slavery, ants and, 14–15
Smokey Bear campaign, success of,
  88–90
snakeheads, 91
soil, benefits of worms to, 16–18
Spathius spp., 70, 71
spiracles, 22
starlings, European, 64–67
Su, Nan-Yao, 80–81
subterranean termites. *See* Formosan
  subterranean termites
sugarcane, cane toads and, 31–32
swamp eels, in Everglades, 84–85

T

Tennessee, wild boars in, 56
termites, 13–14. *See also* Formosan
  subterranean termites
termiticides, 79–80, 94
terpenes, 34
Tetrastichus spp, 71
TGE (transmissible gastroenteritis), 66
Thelohania solenopsae, 46–47
Those Amazing Insects, 11

tortoises, 19
tourism, 52–53, 59
toxicants, 54, 67
trapping, 53–54, 67
travel, species spread and, 59
Tree Bar, 52
treesnakes. *See* brown treesnakes
trout, 84

U

USDA, 27–28, 37, 94

V

venom, 33, 50, 53
vertebrates, defined, 10
vetiver, termite control and, 80
viceroy butterflies, 24
village weaverbirds, 21
virtual modeling, 80–81
viruses, starlings and, 66
voles, wild boars and, 60
volicitin, 34

W

Waldbauer, Gilbert, 13–14
wasps, 16, 35
weaverbirds, 21
well baby appeals, 87
Whittaker, Robert H., 8–9
wild boars. *See* boars
wildlife careers, 92–93
Wildlife Services program, 49
Wilson, E.O., 49
wolves, reintroduction of, 49
Wormbulance, 16–17
worms, 16–18, 29–30

Y

Yellowstone National Park, 84

ABOUT THE AUTHOR

Suellen May writes for agricultural and environmental publications. She is a graduate of the University of Vermont (B.S.) and Colorado State University (M.S.). She has worked in the environmental field for 15 years, including invasive species management for Larimer County Open Lands in Colorado. She served as the Education Committee chairperson for the Colorado Weed Management Association. While living in Fort Collins, Colorado, she founded the Old Town Writers' Group. She lives with her son, Nate, in Bucks County, Pennsylvania. Readers can reach her at suellen0829@yahoo.com.